ISRAEL III

FINDING ANCIENT ISRAEL AMONG THE MODERN NATIONS

K. J. FROLANDER

ISRAEL III: Finding Ancient Israel Among the Modern Nations
Copyright © 2014 by K. J. Frolander

All rights reserved. No part of this book may be reproduced or transmitted in any form or by any means without written permission from the author.

All scripture used in accordance with copyright law. Unless otherwise designated, version is NKJV: Scripture taken from the New King James Version® Copyright © 1982 by Thomas Nelson, Inc. Used by permission. All rights reserved.
All other versions are designated at their use. NIV: THE HOLY BIBLE, NEW INTERNATIONAL VERSION®, NIV® Copyright © 1973, 1978, 1984, 2011 by Biblica, Inc.® Used by permission. All rights reserved worldwide.; GW: GOD'S WORD®, © 1995 God's Word to the Nations. Used by permission of Baker Publishing Group.; NLT: Holy Bible, New Living Translation copyright © 1996, 2004, 2007 by Tyndale House Foundation. Used by permission of Tyndale House Publishers Inc., Carol Stream, Illinois 60188. All rights reserved.

Author photograph © by Deborah Beechy, Columbus, Ohio.
Israel III cover photos taken by Kim Frolander, front cover Sea of Galillee, back cover, Beit Shean ruins; Cover designed & formatted by Janis Teller at Chelsea2583@hotmail.com. British coat of arms photo © Greta Zefo June 2014.

ISBN 978-0-9903059-1-0
Printed in USA

Acknowledgements

Thanks to my Inverness Vineyard Church Israel small group students who helped me refine this final project by asking the most terrific questions.

Special thanks to my beta readers: Monique Whitehead, Julie Gardner, Janna Sturdivant, and Randa Woodward. I really appreciate all your input, advice, comments, questions and encouragement.

To Yeshua, a special thank you for never losing track of any one of us. Your attentive affections overwhelm my soul. You are my Great Champion!

Table of Contents

Acknowledgements 3
Introduction 7
Part 1: The History of Israel and Judah Together 11
  1. The Shared History of Israel 13
  2. Update on the Ten Lost Tribes of Israel 29
  3. Identifying 10-Israel Part A 49
        First issue of disappearance: Simeon 56
  4. Identifying 10-Israel Part B 75
Part 2: Ideas on Where Specific Tribes can be found Today . 83
  5. Gad and Reuben 85
  6. Dan and Benjamin 93
  7. Naphtali and Asher 109
  8. Issachar and Zebulon 123
  9. Levi 135
  10. The House of Joseph: Ephraim and Manasseh 145
  11. Identifying Judah 177
  12. Implications of the Lost Tribes Found 187
  End Notes 197

List of Maps

Map 1: Israel Circa 1991 27
Map 2: Tribal Inheritance of Israel 28
Map 3: Scythian and Parthian Territories circa 100 BC 73
Map 4: Ancient Phoenician Empire 74
Map 5: The Movements of 10-Israel 82
Map 6: Modern Europe..84
Map 7: Iceland Between the Shoulders 108
Map 8: Ephraim and Manasseh by county in England 167

Introduction
and Notes from the Author

If you are picking up this book and being introduced for the first time to the prophesied re-born nation of Israel, I recommend reading the foundational information in *Israel Basics: What Every Christian Should Know* and *Israel II: Beyond the Basics* first so you will have a frame of reference for the material presented in this book.

The question of "What about Israel?" has plagued church leaders for centuries, just as "What about the Gentiles?" pushed the Jewish leaders to think outside what they accepted as normal in the first century AD.

This book contains an overview of the quiet story that God has allowed to be hidden in these last centuries as His Ultimate Plan has been unfolding toward the Last Great Day. There are many details that span the millennia which will be glossed over here.

I encourage you to study Israel in order to learn more about the God we love and serve. Israel, past and present, is a picture of how God interacts with mankind as a nation, just as Jesus is the flesh and blood picture of how God longs to interact with individuals.

There is coming a day, an actual date, one with a sunrise and sunset, which will be the Last Great Day. It will be the greatest day and worst of all days! On that day God is going to have to do some very hard things. We are not going to understand His decisions; likely, we won't agree with His decisions. He will be separating His sheep from the goats. That day will start the eternal reward and damnation of mankind, for actual people. It is going to be a very hard day for Him. And we have a hard decision to make.

Our hard decision has to be this: to trust Him with the hard things that He will have to do.

We are not holy as He is holy, even if we are trying. We are not worthy like He is worthy, even if we are trying. He is the only One capable of making these difficult decisions.

In the days leading up to that Last Great Day, there will be some pretty miserable days here on earth. God promised to lead those who are submitted to Him in those days. Israel in the wilderness is a prophetic picture of what those days will be like. God will provide all we need, but the days will not be easy ones.

The devastation of the earth, the water, the animals, the people, even children will make our hearts groan with the waste. (That waste is only an outward manifestation of what has been going on in the heart of man age after age.) We won't understand when a million people or more die at once in natural disasters like earthquakes, tornadoes and tsunamis, when there is no clean water to drink and there is nowhere to go to get away from the retched stink of rotting flesh. We will know that God could have stopped it, yet He does not. We will mourn for life as we knew it.

It will be nearly impossible in those days to accept God as the loving God we've been taught that He is. He will not appear loving when life is up-rooted, sifted and destroyed.

However, even in the destruction, God is being faithful to His Word. He warned us that this day would come. He will be looking for those who will be found faithful to the End.

Something that I have noticed about people is this: they tend to have their own ideas, spoken or not, and when something doesn't line up with those ideas, they toss out everything they believed as a lie. The better thing is to adjust their original ideas to the truth of experience. It is much easier to toss out the whole idea than humble ourselves to find out where we missed it, as can be seen from the arrogant, godless society in which we live.

If, in those days of horror at the end, we choose the easier way, we may decide we must have been wrong about God altogether. We may decide He doesn't exist, or if He does, He certainly is not in control, and if he is in control, He certainly does not love us. Then all hope is lost.

Wouldn't it be better to go ahead and decide that there will be areas where we will just be wrong about what we thought it would look like? Jewish scholars and prophets spent centuries studying and interpreting the scriptures about Jesus' first coming, and much of Israel missed Him. Why do we think we will be any different? Why don't we make the decision before the persecution begins to trust the decisions that He makes as just. Our society has been begging for justice for decades, centuries maybe. It is coming. *He* is coming. But it will not be the justice we had in mind when we asked. Let's choose now to trust His justice as right. There is no one who can make the decisions He will have to make. May our hearts honor His decisions in that Day!

One of the major thermometers or plumb lines God uses to test the nations even today, before the great terror begins, is how we treat Israel.

> **Genesis 12:3** I will bless those who bless you and curse those who curse you.

Jerusalem will be a trembling cup that will push nations to a decision on whether they will support Israel or denounce her (Zechariah 12:2).

Unfortunately, the next verse (12:3) says that all nations will rise against Israel. In fact, we already see this happening. However, just because our nation's leadership doesn't support Israel, does not mean that we, personally, can't support her, financially, vocally, helping those among us who are of Israel and those living in the land. God will give us opportunities to support or reject His People, Israel. We must be watching for them as more and more nations begin to curse them.

This book, like all others, has an agenda. My agenda is simple: uncover and expose God's faithfulness to His Word throughout the ages and show that He has not forgotten or "lost" any part of Israel. The underlying premise that we can trust Him is the basis of the deep relationship required to function as part of the living, breathing Bride of Christ in those horrific final days. Oh, that we would become a Bride worthy of the Son!

This maturity in relationship moves beyond the current growth stage of the Bride. We are still getting comfortable with being healed, physically and emotionally, and getting used to being a people of prayer and worship. The stage of the Church being birthed now is the Bride understanding and supporting Israel as our brother, and yet more than a brother, because Christianity was never intended to be separated from Judaism. We were always intended to be one. Now this concept is called the One New Man. But we have lived separately so long, only God can teach us to be one again.

PART 1

THE HISTORY OF JUDAH AND ISRAEL TOGETHER

God's story of Israel begins with Abraham responding "yes" to His call to come out of Ur of the Chaldees and go to a land He had prepared for him. Their story has continued over 3,500 years since that day. There have been some high highs and some terrible lows in those millennia. But one thing remains constant: God loves His people, Israel.

1

THE SHARED HISTORY OF ISRAEL

There is a systematic and not-so-hidden scheme to remove God from modernity. The agenda used to be more hidden than the blatant degradation of godliness performed today. This plan has been around since the beginning. It is Satan's agenda which he plants into human minds. His goal is to supplant God and take as much of what belongs to God with him as possible. Modernly, this agenda is perpetuated by the ever increasing love of self found in humanism.

Humanism sets up you—your needs and desires—as the god before which you bow daily. What better way for Satan to usurp God's rightful worship than to channel it toward something we were designed to care for: ourselves?

The way in which Satan perpetuates humanism is to promote God as a dusty relic leftover from a pre-enlightened age and set up science and thinking outside boundaries as the new standard by which to measure progress and success. Through people, Satan has tried to do away with God's boundaries for righteous living and has rewritten history with his own emphasis that diminishes God's role not only in the development and rule of the nations, but also in our everyday individual lives.

History

Most Christians are aware of the concept of "the Lost Tribes of Israel." If not, a simple Google search will well-inform the unaware, as everyone from *Encyclopaedia Britannica* to Wikipedia has an article about these mystical people "lost" to the pages of history. When discussed, the Lost Tribes are usually referenced in one of two ways: whispers that connote the idea that people who are disobedient will be wiped out by God, even if they are "chosen," so watch your back. Or they are talked about in arrogant tones that belittle the Lost Tribes as if "maybe you'd have gotten to come back if you had believed in Jesus, but you lost your last chance."

However, the concept of the Lost Tribes is a fairly new concept, that has been perpetuated in the last 150-200 years by history books that dropped certain civilizations and pushed the history of others as the only thing that was going on in the world at a particular time. For example, have you ever noticed that both Chinese and Japanese culture and history have existed successfully for thousands and thousands of years, and yet we in the West don't usually study of their history? We newcomers to the world scene, in America especially, can be very short sighted. A dynasty is not winning three national football championships in a row, it is 300 to 3,000 years of the same ruling family, of continued history, and yet we in the West study nothing about it as we read history, so we discount it as having no influence and therefore find it unimportant. Our nation has not even been around 250 years yet!

A civilization cannot be important if they didn't put it in our history book, right? Wrong!

SATAN'S GOAL AND PLAN: MAKE GOD A LIAR

Satan's goal is to take God's place, receive His worship as the Worthy One. But God is God; He holds all the cards; He created the cards. Many people through the ages have chosen to go Satan's way, because it seemed easier, more fun, or provided them more power here on earth. However there have always been a people, called "a remnant of righteousness," who have chosen God and His way of life. Their genealogy can be seen in Genesis 5 and Matthew 1. Those righteous men began just carrying a seed of a promised Messiah, passed through their generations, which resulted in a flesh and blood Savior of the world: Yeshua.

The size of the remnant of righteousness has waxed and waned through the centuries. And the promise of God for the people of the Covenant has grown to include more blessings as it has been revealed from time to time. For example Adam to Noah to Abraham to David to Jesus, at each revelation of the covenant more was revealed, and the Covenant got bigger and better and more complex. It also got easier to break, because the new revelations of the Covenant dealt with not just our outward actions, but our motivations and our thoughts.

However, the *only* thing Satan has to do to "win" is to get God to break even one iota of His side of the Covenant. If that were to happen, then this whole redemption plan would unravel and Satan would have legal authority to take over. So Satan's plan is very simple: force God into breaking His Word or promise.

The main items of the Covenant include a sinless savior for the people who is a blessing to the whole earth, a blessed people, the Promised Land to specific borders belonging to a specific people, and a king from the line of David.

In the beginning, Satan tried to destroy God's promise of a nation made of Abraham's children by enslaving them in Egypt. That didn't work, so he tried to take them out of the Promised Land by inspiring first the

Assyrians then the Babylonians to conquer Israel and Judah between 722 and 500 BC. That didn't work, so he tried to kill Jesus. But Jesus wouldn't stay dead! So Satan tried to wipe the chosen people off the face of the earth using the Spanish Inquisition in the 1490's and Hitler's Nazis in the 1930's and 1940's. Nearly 1/3 of the Jews survived Hitler and Satan's plot. Not only did that horrific plan not work, it brought the Jews back into their own Promised Land! So Satan stirred up the nations surrounding Israel into war five times to try to take away the Promised Land and push the Jews into the sea, and every time, Israel won the war and gained land! So that didn't work. (When well-meaning Christians ask, "But what about the poor Palestinians?" they are buying into the lie of the enemy that God won't provide for both. He already did: space for "Palestinians" is called Jordan.) All of these attempts of Satan are trying to destroy one aspect of the Covenant or another to make God incapable of fulfilling His end of the agreement, therefore becoming a liar and acting in contrast to His character. It is Satan's long term agenda, but it's never going to happen!

When God made His promises to the seed of Abraham, He included all the tribes of Israel. Currently, the Jews living in Israel only consist of *some* of the people from the tribes of Judah, Benjamin, and Levi. More members of these three tribes are still scattered in the earth today, and most of them know who they are. But there are many more descendants from the tribes of the northern Kingdom of Israel who are not represented in the new nation of Israel. Where are Dan, Issachar, Simeon, Zebulon, Asher, Naphtali, Ephraim and Manasseh? Did God lose them or reject them when they left the land of Israel at the time of the Assyrian invasion? No. However, this simple answer begs two questions: Where are they? and Do they know who they are?

As an aside: Every time God makes a promise, He is putting everything on the line. He must fulfill every promise, every word He speaks! This applies to personal promises too. It is critical that we understand the importance of accurately hearing and believing the promises God makes to us, especially when we relay those promise words to others. The book of Hebrews tells us of the men who God says had great faith. Many of them did not see their promises fulfilled in their lifetimes because the promises were so huge, like Abraham's descendants being as many as the stars of the sky and the sands of the seashore. But we are living in those promises fulfilled today! Because God always fulfills His Word!

FROM VICTORIAN ERA FORWARD

Historically, people from the 10 tribes living in the northern Kingdom of Israel (10-Israel) knew who they were. Those living among the nations could sometimes even trace back their tribal heritage to a particular son of Jacob. It is recorded in their national founding histories and folklore. But beginning with the rise of modern-day humanism during the "Enlightenment" of the 1700's, both of which are steeped in the Theory of Evolution, things started to change. Satan's plan includes wiping out every trace of history that points to the Bible being true. A huge chunk of truth in the Bible is that there are an historical 12 tribes of Israel. They have actual progeny walking around today. If we just call them "the Jews" it takes away from them actually being the Israel of the Bible, from the tribe of Judah or Benjamin, Issachar or Manasseh. If historians are bent to accept and emphasize certain histories of civilizations over others, the others tend to get lost to modernity, since history keeps moving forward.

Satan's agenda to make God look like a fairy tale and sweep Him and His dusty old faithfulness aside for shiny new scientific ways of thinking is working for most of the world's population. Satan has been able to remove the fear of God that was present in Western society for hundreds and hundreds of years.

> **Psalm 36:1** NLT Sin whispers to the wicked, deep within their hearts. They have no fear of God at all.

If someone was not raised as a Believer or has not had a significant encounter with the Living God—whether through a revelation, dream or another person—they don't even need to buy into Satan's lie for it to be the place of "truth" from which they live. It is "normal" now. But something being normal and accepted does not make it truth.

There is a story being played out in the earth, and in the end, all will be revealed. Truth will win, because He created the "game."

Satan's Agenda in Daily Headlines:

Holocaust Denial

December 16, 2005, Douglas Birch reported in *The Baltimore Sun* article, "Iranian president makes pitch to radicals," "When Iranian President Mahmoud Ahmadinejad called the Holocaust a 'myth' this week, he wasn't only embracing one of the key tenets of modern anti-Semitism."[1]

Abortion on Demand

April 25, 2007, Oscar Avilia writing for *The Chicago Tribune* reports in an article titled, "Lawmakers legalize abortion within Mexico City," "Lawmakers voted Tuesday to legalize abortions in the Mexican capital during the first 12 weeks of pregnancy, capping a heated debate in a Roman Catholic nation that now will have one of Latin America's most liberal abortion policies."[2]

No School Prayer

March 21, 2012, Hugh Willett of Knoxnews.com out of Knoxville, Tennessee published the article, "Lenoir City school system curtailing prayers at public meetings" reporting, "The Lenoir City School Board has ceased opening its meetings with a prayer in a response to secular organizations who allege that prayer at board meetings and other school functions violates the Constitution."[3]

Evolution

April 3, 2010, Richard Gray of the UK's *The Telegraph* wrote in an article called, "Missing link between man and apes found," "The new species of hominid, the evolutionary branch of primates that includes humans, is to be revealed when the two-million-year-old skeleton of a child is unveiled this week."

Just from a simple search of article titles, it is evident that our world's trajectory is on a path toward ultimate destruction. More issues that Satan is twisting into worldwide cultural change include:
- Spiritual leaders brought down by sin
- Lawlessness in the U.S. and other national governments
- Gay marriage acceptance
- School shootings and beheadings
- Sex trafficking

WHAT WILL HAPPEN?

As history progresses toward the End, what will happen? First, Israel will be restored as a nation among the nations (Ezekiel 36 & 37). This natural birth of a nation happened May 14-15, 1948, yet the spiritual restoration of Israel still needs completion. Romans 8:22 and Matthew 24 tell us that creation will groan and quake for her Maker to restore righteousness, that there will be wars and rumors of wars, and lawlessness will abound. In the End all nations will turn away from Israel. They will gather together against her as to destroy her (Revelation 16:14, 16). However on that day, God Himself will avenge Israel and come to rescue her (Ez 37:18-33). The two million man army (Rev 9:16) will be wiped out, birds will feast on their flesh (Rev 19:18-21), and it will take seven months of continuous work by teams to bury them all (Ez 39:12-14) and seven years to burn all their weapons (Ez 39:9).

Yet Israel shall remain.

GOD'S CHARACTER

We see God's character of faithfulness through the entire scripture. When He says He will do something, He does it. Sometimes He offers an option, as in the case of Nineveh. God sent Jonah to call the people to repentance in order to avoid His wrath. Nineveh heeded the warning, repented and was spared.

God is kind, loving, generous, good, and yet firm, jealous—the good kind of jealous—just, and vengeful in equal measure. That is scary. Since God sent Jesus, mankind has been living in the age of His grace, knowing His love for two millennia now, but there is coming a day when His wrath will be satisfied. In His love, He told us what to look for ahead of time in His Word. (One of those signs is a completely restored Israel.)

> **NINEVEH UPDATE**
> The Assyrian city of Nineveh was located just across the Tigris River from modern-day city of Mosel, Iraq.[6] With the 2014 rise of ISIS in Iraq which has murdered or kicked out all the Christians in Mosel, it will be interesting to see if/when God removes His hand that stayed the curses he spoke against this ancient city.

He will faithfully execute His just judgment over the earth and only the purified gold, silver and precious jewels of our works of obedience can stand in His wake. (I Corinthians 3:9-15)

תא

ISRAEL'S OVERVIEW FROM ITS INCEPTION

God chose Abraham and promised to make him the father of great nations and one special nation, which later would be named Israel. Abraham entered into covenant with God, and the children of Abraham have been receiving the blessings of God ever since. They have also lived under curses when they have not followed God's covenant which they agreed to.

During the initial covenant agreement (Genesis 15) Abraham prepared the animals as God told him by cleaving them in half and letting the blood pool between them. It was the way covenants were cut. According to ancient tradition, the greater party walked through the blood first and then the lesser party of the covenant followed, effectively saying, "I know this being cleaved in half is what will happen to me if I ever break this covenant with you, even if keeping the covenant costs me death." Their blood spattered clothing served as a reminder of this unbreakable agreement. (Death was the only way to finish the obligation of a covenant).

In the covenant with Abraham, God, as the greater party, passed through the blood first; He was the smoking oven and the burning torch (Genesis 15:17). He was the only party that passed through, effectively saying, "If I break this covenant with you, I will pay for it with my life; if you break this covenant I will pay for it with my life." What god has ever made an offer like that? Only One!

One of the consequences of not following the covenant agreement was that Israel would be exiled from the Promised Land. Unfortunately, Israel was unable to keep the covenant. After cycles of war skirmishes, repentance, and relapsing back into sin, God allowed the nation of Israel to be ripped in two, just like those sacrifices were cleaved so many years ago.

The Split After Solomon

Israel's split occurred after King Solomon's reign. The northern kingdom was called Israel, and consisted of 10 tribes who were ruled in the first generation by one of Solomon's servants, Jeroboam. The southern kingdom was called Judah and consisted of the tribes of Judah, Benjamin and some of Levi. They were ruled by a man from the line of David, Rehoboam.

These two kingdoms have not been reunited even to this day.

According to Revelation though, there will be unity in Israel again before the final Great Day. Both Revelation 7 and 14 mention that 144,000 people of Israel will be sealed and stand on Mount Zion together with Jesus. Specifically, there will be 12,000 from *each* tribe.

This is a beautiful promise of God that is yet to be fulfilled, and it looks in the natural as if God will have trouble fulfilling it since 10 of the tribes are "missing." Based on the way God has fulfilled every promise in the past though, we shouldn't worry. Until 70 years ago, it didn't look like Israel could ever exist as a modern nation, since the Jews were scattered all across the globe, and yet despite five major wars on their Promised Land, Israel stands strong as a nation once again!

Israel and Judah are not synonyms in the Bible

It is important to state what might be obvious when you actually stop to put words to it, but it may have been a bit scrambled in your mind—as it was mine. "Israel" and "Judah" both in word and in the people the words represent are not synonyms. They are not interchangeable. Especially after Solomon when the nation was cleaved into two kingdoms. When scripture says "Judah," it means the southern kingdom of Judah, the people who remained under the throne of David's heir. When scripture says "Israel," it means Israel, the people of the northern tribes. From here on out these people will be referred to as 10-Israel in order to preserve the difference in our minds. When "Israel" is used I am referring to the man Israel/Jacob, the physical land/nation/state of Israel, or the original full kingdom. Context should make it obvious. For 2,900-3,000 years Judah and 10-Israel have been distinct entities on earth, but God will bring them back together as one in the final days.

In the year of this writing, 2014, the Land of Israel has been back in Jewish hands for 66 years, since 1948. The return of the Lord could not have happened before then because of the prophecies in Zechariah 12:2-9 and 14: 1-4 and Jesus confirming in Matthew 24:15 that Daniel's prophecy about the sacrifices being cut off in Daniel 11:31 being a future event, among many others.[7] But now, the return is prophetically on track. The current Jewish population of Israel (75.1%), though predominately secular, stands at just over six million souls.⁵ However we know that historically those Jews predominately trace their heritage back to only 2-3 tribes: Judah, Benjamin and Levi.*

Since the current Jewish population only represents portions of three tribes, what about the other tribes as prophesied in scripture? They must also be represented in Greater Israel, trusting Yeshua as their Messiah, and in numbers as large as 12,000 if we look at scripture literally, and more than 12,000 if we look at the number symbolically or figuratively, since *12* represents the number of "government and leadership" and *1,000* represents "fullness." (If we use 12,000 as a symbol, it should represent the 12 tribes governing in their completeness.)

The question then arises, where did the other tribes go? In the last 150-200 years—the only history we collectively have known for six or so generations—the other tribes have been referred to as the "Ten Lost Tribes of Israel." Funnily enough, we can't even agree on which tribes make up the ten.

ISRAELIS

The real confusion comes in when today we call the Jews living in the Promised Land, "Israelis," because the people living there are for the most part from Judah or Benjamin or Levi (previously "Judea"), while the people from 10-Israel are still abroad in exile.

---

*Concerning Levi: Because they did not inherit land, the Levities dwelt all over the land, a few towns in each tribal allotment were set aside for Levi. This continued for all their generations. When Israel split into two kingdoms after Solomon's reign, Judah and Benjamin were the only two tribes represented in the Southern Kingdom of Judah. The other 10 tribes were the Northern Kingdom of Israel. This remained the dividing line for centuries until the Assyrian (722 BC) and then Babylonian (586 BC) invasions into the north and the south, respectively. After 70 years in exile the Kingdom of Judah re-formed in their previously held land. About 10% of the Jewish population in exile returned, leaving 90% abroad. The 90% did make pilgrimages back to Israel for Feast days occasionally, but maintained their homes and lives in foreign lands

In the biblical text after the historical split, when the names Ephraim, Israel, Joseph, Jacob or Manasseh are used, the scripture is referring to 10-Israel. When the Bible says Judah, Judea, David, or Zion it is referring to Judah, from which we get the name "Jews." When both are mentioned, especially in prophecy, it means both. Again, the names are not interchangeable or synonyms. Jeremiah 31 is a perfect example of this difference. "Ephraim my firstborn" (Jeremiah 31:9) and "Judah" (Jeremiah 31:23) are referring to the two separate peoples with two different national paths. God's use of "my people" refers to both 10-Israel and Judah.

God distinguishes between the two entities of His people twice in the same chapter of Jeremiah, so they are clearly separate in His mind.

> **Jeremiah 31:23** "Behold, the days are coming, says the LORD, that I will sow the house of Israel and the house of Judah with the seed of man and the seed of beast.
>
> **Jeremiah 31:31** "Behold, the days are coming, says the LORD, when I will make a new covenant with the house of Israel and with the house of Judah—

But one day the broken branch of the house of Israel and the house of Judah shall be restored as one branch.

> **Jeremiah 3:18 NIV** "Behold, the days are coming, says the LORD, when I will make a new covenant with the house of Israel and with the house of Judah.
>
> **Ezekiel 37:15-22** [15] Again the word of the LORD came to me, saying, [16] "As for you, son of man, take a stick for yourself and write on it: 'For Judah and for the children of Israel, his companions.' Then take another stick and write on it, 'For Joseph, the stick of Ephraim, and *for* all the house of Israel, his companions.' [17] Then join them one to another for yourself into one stick, and they will become one in your hand.
> [18] "And when the children of your people speak to you, saying, 'Will you not show us what you *mean* by

these?'— ¹⁹ say to them, 'Thus says the Lord GOD: "Surely I will take the stick of Joseph, which *is* in the hand of Ephraim, and the tribes of Israel, his companions; and I will join them with it, with the stick of Judah, <u>and make them one stick, and they will be one in My hand</u>."' ²⁰ And the sticks on which you write will be in your hand before their eyes.

²¹ "Then say to them, 'Thus says the Lord GOD: "Surely I will take the children of Israel from among the nations, wherever they have gone, and will gather them from every side and bring them into their own land; ²² and I will make them one nation in the land, on the mountains of Israel; and one king shall be king over them all; <u>they shall no longer be two nations, nor shall they ever be divided into two kingdoms again.</u>

THE FIRST DIASPORA OF ISRAEL

A couple of hundred years after Israel split in two, 10-Israel came under attack from Assyria. In three waves over 20 years, the people living in 10-Israel were carted off as slaves to Assyria and were resettled in communities there. Between attacks though, many families and communities of 10-Israel left of their own free will and immigrated to other places.

JUDAH'S PUNISHMENT AND RETURN

The same ousting from the Land happened to Judah 137 years later. The Babylonians came in and conquered them, carrying them away captive. However, this time, God promised that after 70 years, they would be allowed to return to the Promised Land. (Jeremiah 25:11-12). It happened, exactly as God said it would!

However, the whole company of Judah did not obey and return after their exile was complete. Only about 10% returned to the land. For various reasons 90% of Judah remained where they were among the nations; they lived in concentrated communities east of the Promised Land in Babylon (current day Iraq).

JUDAH IN THE LAND AND 10-ISRAEL OUTSIDE THE LAND

After partial Judah returned to the Land, they rebuilt their nation as God said they would. However from their return until 1948, they always functioned under someone else's authority. Judah did not live under self rule for 2,500 years!

After about 500 years of the people of Judah being horribly rebellious subjects, the Roman rulers had taken as much of Judah's revolting as they were going to, and they crushed Judah in 70-72 AD. No stone was left upon another.

The 10% of Judah which had returned was mostly killed, but some escaped abroad or were relocated in the Roman Empire. However the other 90% of Judah and all of 10-Israel were still scattered abroad, intact. But where are they now?

Because they kept following the Torah, most of scattered Judah know who they are and readily identify as Children of the Covenant. But what about 10-Israel? They've currently been gone from their land for 2,700 years? For the most part today, they do not know their identity as Israelites.

FINDING 10-ISRAEL

Obviously God has not "lost" the 10 tribes of Israel, but how should we go about looking for 10-Israel? There are two particular scripture descriptions of the tribes. One is found in Genesis 49 from when Jacob is dying and prophetically describes his 12 sons and who they would become in the future. The second description is given by Moses in the form of a blessing; it is recorded in Deuteronomy 33.

When we study these two passages, they become a road map which describes what characteristics and even what locations we should look for in the Last Days to find 10-Israel!

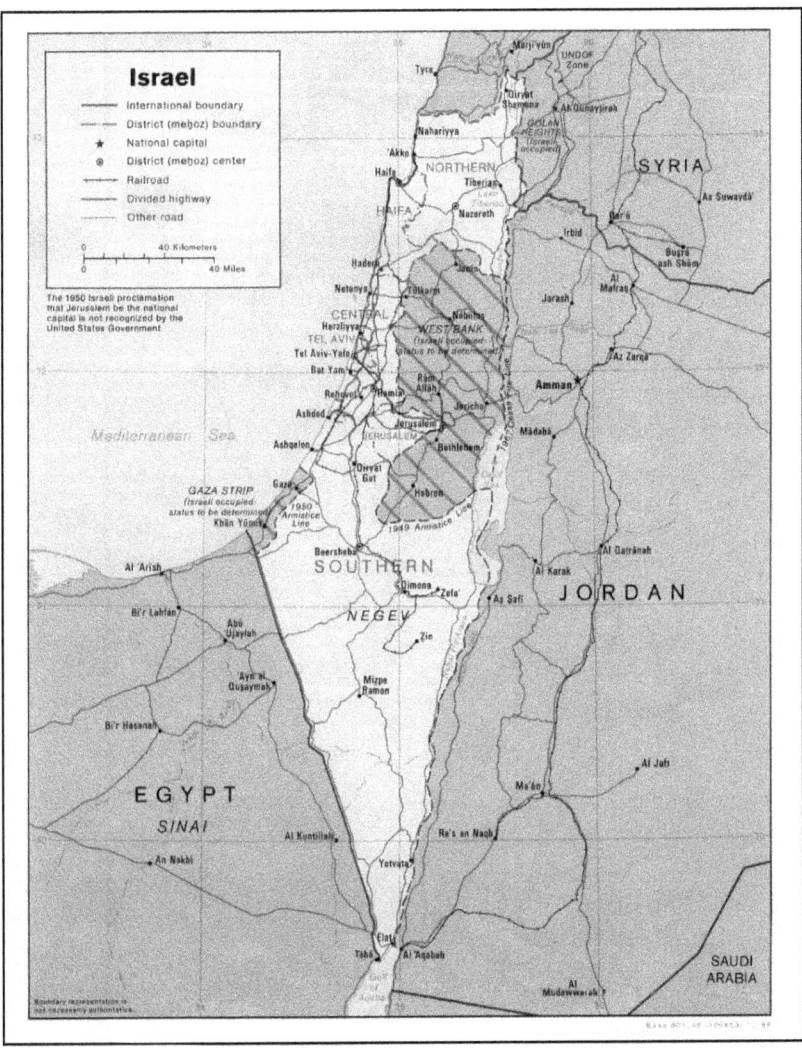

MAP 1: ISRAEL CIRCA 2003.
Notes: This map shows the current day boundaries, large cities, bodies of water and a few of the main highways in Israel. The horizontal lines drawn over the West Bank and Gaza indicate that land as Palestinian and Arab held land. The countries surrounding Israel are in a darker shade and are all Arab-led nations. Map courtesy of Free US CIA Factbook © 2008 maps by Michael Meuser at Mapcruzin.com

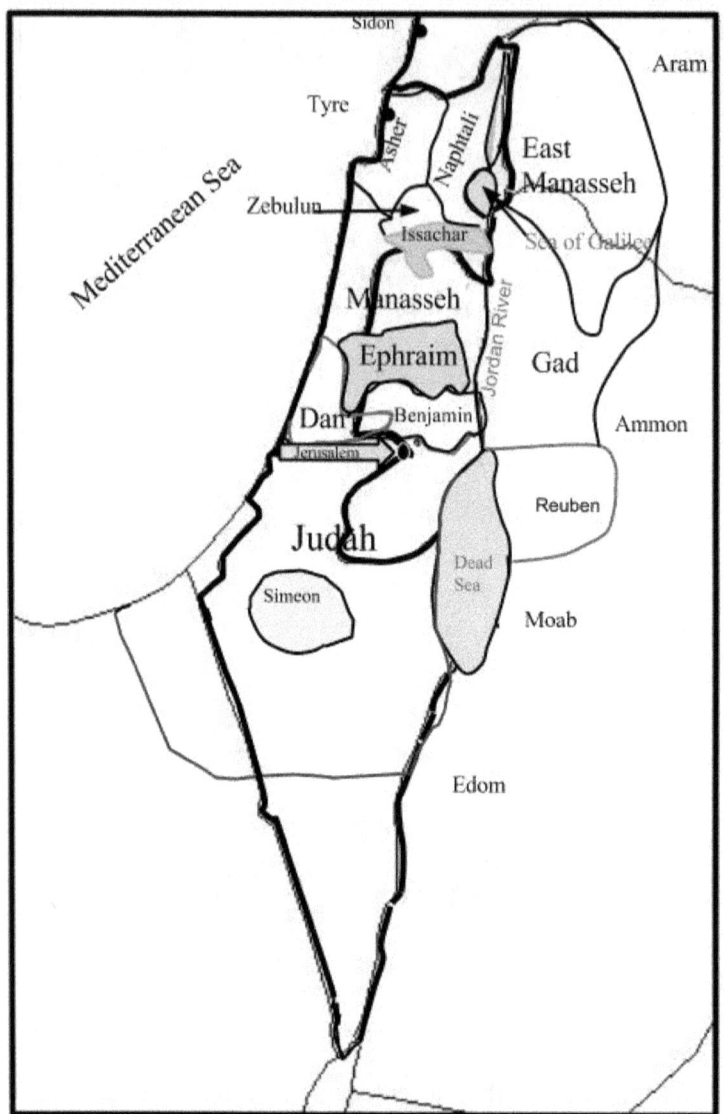

MAP 2: MAP OF TRIBAL INHERITANCE

Notes: Outline is of the modern State of Israel, 2014 and corresponds to Map 1. This map is circa the time of Joshua and the judges ~1200 BC. Levi had no inheritance of land. East ½ Manasseh, Gad and Reuben are all located in what is now Jordan on the east side of the Jordan River. Manasseh, Ephraim, Benjamin, and part of Judah inherited land which is currently the Arab-held West Bank.

2

UPDATE ON THE TEN LOST TRIBES OF ISRAEL

Author note: Before starting to research this topic, I had no idea what a balygon (chaos) of information is available out there. Many sources on the Web are trying to rewrite history, especially the history of the Jews. The main thing is to know that God never lost track of the tribes of the people who bear His name.

FOUNDATION

To begin on fairly undisputed ground, the Bible teaches and non-wikipedia historians agree: Abraham begat Isaac, who begat Jacob, who had 12 sons. They got stuck in Egypt, where they multiplied rapidly and were made slaves. God brought them out and made them into their own nation called Israel. The size of the group varies from 600,000 to 3 million. That is 72 persons to 600,000+ in 400 years. The original Promised Land of Israel was located in the exact place as the current State of Israel. (The boundaries are much more firm today than then.) The Israelites, also called Hebrews, set up housekeeping in their own God-directed plots of land in the Promised Land, and they were governed by a combination of Torah, Judges and Prophets for 450 years (Acts 13:20) before they demanded a king. The first three kings (known as the Golden Age of Israel's history) lasted 120 years (40 years for each king). Then Israel was split/cleaved into two kingdoms, north and south, called Israel and Judah respectively. Both kingdoms continued through a succession of their own kings for many generations. There were 19 kings of Israel in the north, until 722 BC when they were conquered and carried away, or fled ahead of the invading Assyrian army. There were 20 kings of Judah who ruled for a greater average number of years, until 586 BC when the Babylonians came and carried them away into captivity. What happened to them all?

And here the controversy begins.

There are two basic theories as to where the 10 lost tribes went: the large view and the small view. We will start with the small view of pockets of Hebrews being found throughout the earth, because, well, it's smaller.

Fast forward to the End for why it's important

There are two main reasons identifying Israel is important. First, in the final Last Days (as opposed to just the last thousand years or so) the earth and all people on it will be in dire straits. Even God says we wouldn't survive if He hadn't shortened the days (Matt 24:22; Mark 13:20). You know if <u>God</u> says it will be hard, it's gonna be ROUGH!

God promised that He would rescue people who call on His name and set up His kingdom; He also promised to never forget Israel, that she is engraved on the palm of His hand. (Isaiah 49:16: The Hebrew word translated "engraved" here, is more precisely "hacked" which is pretty strong language!) If God "lost" ten of the twelve tribes, even if you claim it was their own disobedience that "disqualified" them, how can God be trusted to fulfill the rest of His Word? It is imperative that we trust God, and more trust will be needed in those final days than ever before. It is a tremendous boost to our faith when we see God keep His promises through the ages, again and again and again!

Secondly, in Revelation 7, after the 6th seal has been opened, there are four angels at the four corners of the earth holding back the four winds. Then an angel cries with a loud voice,

> "Do not harm the earth, the sea, or the trees till we have sealed the servants of our God on their foreheads." And I heard the number of those who were sealed. One hundred *and* forty-four thousand of all the tribes of the children of Israel *were* sealed: of the tribe of Judah twelve thousand *were* sealed;
> of the tribe of Reuben twelve thousand *were* sealed;
> of the tribe of Gad twelve thousand *were* sealed;
> 6 of the tribe of Asher twelve thousand *were* sealed;
> of the tribe of Naphtali twelve thousand *were* sealed;
> of the tribe of Manasseh twelve thousand *were* sealed;
> 7 of the tribe of Simeon twelve thousand *were* sealed;
> of the tribe of Levi twelve thousand *were* sealed;
> of the tribe of Issachar twelve thousand *were* sealed;
> 8 of the tribe of Zebulun twelve thousand *were* sealed;
> of the tribe of Joseph twelve thousand *were* sealed;
> of the tribe of Benjamin twelve thousand *were* sealed."
> (Revelation 7:3-8)

These last four verses explain that the 144,000 to be sealed will be divided equally among the 12 Tribes of the Children of Israel: Judah, Reuben, Gad, Asher, Naphtali, Manasseh, Simeon, Levi, Issachar, Zebulon, Joseph and Benjamin. Twelve thousand from each tribe. Revelation discusses these sealed 144,000 of Israel again:

> **Revelation 14:18** Then I looked, and behold, a Lamb standing on Mount Zion, and with Him <u>one hundred *and* forty-four thousand, having His Father's name written on their foreheads.</u> 2 And I heard a voice from heaven, like the voice of many waters, and like the voice of loud thunder. And I heard the sound of harpists playing their harps. 3 They sang as it were a new song before the

> throne, before the four living creatures, and the elders; and no one could learn that song except the hundred *and* forty-four thousand who were redeemed from the earth.

So in the End, 144,000 Children of Israel, 12,000 from each tribe, will be sealed for the Lord. They will stand with the Lamb on Mount Zion with their Father's name on their foreheads (usually where people are sealed) and they will sing a new song before the throne and Elders that only they, the redeemed of the earth, know.

OWNERSHIP OF BEING SEALED

To be sealed in the ancient days was putting your stamp of ownership on something. A way of saying something came from you. You may be familiar with the way noblemen used to wear signet rings which they set into warmed wax to seal letters, as if signing them but also to keep people with malicious intent or even just nosey people from tampering with the message contained within.

This scripture seems to say then that the sealed 144,000 will be people who belong to God. More clearly, they will be Messianic Jews in the Land of Israel.

WHO ARE THE TRIBES OF ISRAEL?

The sons of Jacob/Israel is the simple answer to this question. From Genesis 29:31-30:24 & 35:18 in birth order they are as follows: Reuben, Simeon, Levi, Judah, Dan, Naphtali, Gad, Asher, Issachar, Zebulon, Joseph, and Benjamin.

But again, up pops controversy. Joseph was sold into slavery by his brothers (Genesis 39), because it was the Lord's plan to save His people. Joseph had two sons while in Egypt: Manasseh and Ephraim (Genesis 48:1). When it came time to bless and prophesy over Jacob/Israel's sons at his deathbed, all twelve were there, but Jacob also blessed Joseph's sons as if they were his own.

> **Genesis 48:5-6** And now your two sons, Ephraim and Manasseh, who were born to you in the land of Egypt before I came to you in Egypt, *are* mine; as Reuben and Simeon, they shall be mine. ⁶ Your offspring whom you beget after them shall be yours; they will be called by the name of their brothers in their inheritance.

Genesis 49 records the prophecy of blessing Jacob speaks over each of his 12 sons which becomes a set of clues we can use to figure out what happened to the tribes because God always fulfills His Word.

At the Exodus, 400 years after Jacob's prophetic blessing, a strange thing happened among the Hebrews. Of course, the families of these 12 men, plus the two sons of Joseph had multiplied greatly, but because of Reuben's sexual involvement with Jacob's concubine Bilhah, he lost his firstborn status among his brothers. From that time forward Reuben and his sons did not carry the mantle of leadership among the sons of Jacob. When Jacob's daughter Dinah was raped, Jacob's next two sons Simeon and Levi avenged her shame by murdering an entire city full of men (Genesis 34), and their father was displeased with their obnoxious behavior. Later in scripture when the tribes are given their encampment layout, their marching orders, and finally their land inheritances, the tribes are listed not only in other-than-birth-orders, but with different tribes! It is helpful to realize that the 12 tribes of Israel are really 13 tribes, because the "tribe of Joseph" is now referred to as the "house of Joseph" or by his sons' names, the tribes of Manasseh and Ephraim.

In many of the scriptural references there are still 12 tribes listed, usually because the Levites are removed from the list, as they did not receive a land inheritance in the Promised Land, and they encamped surrounding the tabernacle before the other tribes branched out on the four sides. Strangely, three times the tribe of Dan is omitted in the tribal listings, most notably in Revelation 7 (see p. 31) where Joseph and Levi are listed, but Dan and Ephraim are missing). What is that about?

LITTLE RABBIT TRAIL OF THE NAME GAME

What if we look for a deeper, hidden message in the names of the tribes listed in Revelation 7? If we list their names and meanings in order of appearance, in the same way we did with the first 10 generations of Adam through Noah (Chapter 3 in *Israel II: Beyond the Basics*) and found a hidden prophecy of Jesus, what will we find here? [3]

Judah	"I will praise the Lord" or "Let God be praised"
Reuben	"Behold a son" or "Son of vision" "Son who has seen"[6]
Gad	"Good fortune" more precisely "harrowing fortune"[7]
Asher	"Happy am I" or "to go (straight) on because it is highly pleasing to progress"[9]
Naphtali	"My wrestling"
Manasseh	"Making me to forget" or "from a debt" [10]
Simeon	"God hears me" or "He who hears" related to verb Shma (hear & obey)[11]
Levi	"Joined to me"
Issachar	"Purchased me"[13] "Man of hire" "He is wages" or "there is recompense" [12]
Zebulon	"(a bridegroom's gift of) a (glorious) Dwelling (place)"[13]
Joseph	"God will add to me"
Benjamin	"Son of His right hand" (right hand denoting " seat of power")[8]

If we string the meanings together they say, "Let God be praised *for His* Son has seen us *as His* harrowing fortune. I go straight (righteous) because it is highly pleasing to do so. My wrestling *(from going straight)* puts away from *me* a debt *(of sin) because* God hears me *and is* joined to me. *There is also* a recompense *which is* a bridegroom's gift of a glorious dwelling place *which* He will add to me, the son of *His seat of power*, His right hand." (I added the words in italics to complete the thoughts for us Western, Greek thinkers.)

A simpler version with minimized name meanings:[3] "I will praise the Lord *for* He has looked on me *and* granted good fortune. Happy am I *because* my wrestling *God is* making me to forget. God hears me *and is* joined to me. *He has* purchased me a dwelling. God will add to me *the* Son of His right hand."

The tribes left out of this order found in Revelation and their meanings are supplied: Dan[5] means "Judge" which embodies the idea of government, and Ephraim[4] means "I am twice fruitful" or, if Joseph was making a play on words, "Fruitfulness in the land of affliction."

There could be any number of reasons God chose not to list Dan and Ephraim, but chose to include Levi and Joseph in this End Times prophecy, but I don't think it was because they have been forsaken by God and were given up because of their ancient idolatry or current "lostness" as some suggest.[3] I think these two were left out in order to make the "name meanings prophetic statement" we've discovered. Historian/writer Steven M. Collins provides a thought provoking discourse here: http://stevenmcollins.com/WordPress/?p=6120.

WHO ARE THE TEN?

Based on geography and history we conclude that the Northern tribes consisted of the following: Manasseh, Naphtali, Asher, Zebulon, Issachar, Gad, Ephraim, Dan, Reuben, and Simeon.

This leaves the two tribes in the southern Kingdom of Judah: Judah and Benjamin. Simeon is difficult because it is located south of Judah (see map on p. 28).[16] But it is usually found with the northern tribes.

BACK TO THE SMALL VIEW OF FINDING THE TEN LOST TRIBES

Some sources say that 10-Israel has so intermingled with "others," or Gentiles, that they cannot be distinguished and therefore are forever lost. But to deny that they can be found or that they exist actually contradicts the Word of God. "God is on record that they will be here. God gave a whole chapter giving us clues on how we can find them, so it must be important to him that we do identify them."[18]

Various rumors of little pockets of people who have similar worship styles, traditions such as 8th-day circumcision, full beards and side locks, or similar words as the Hebrews have been discovered.

> Groups in Afghanistan, Kurdistan, Iraq, Persia, China, Japan and in various places in Africa, have either claimed descent from the Lost Hebrew Tribes, or have been suggested by travelers or researchers for that distinction. It has even been suggested that some North and South American Indians, as well as the origins of the British people, could be traced to the Lost Tribes of Israel.[14]

Some of those groups with DNA evidence accepted by the Israeli government as genuine include *Beni Yisrael* of West India, *Bene Menashe/Shinlung* from the Burmese border of India, the *Falashas* of Ethiopia, and some men among the Lemba in South Africa.[14] Obviously the Ashkenazi and Sephardic (Spanish) Jews have long known their heritage.

These pocket groups have been discovered, and some have been making *aliyah* [literally meaning "to go up (to Jerusalem)" but used as an idiom for immigrating to Israel]. The Law of Return (identifying people who can receive citizenship in Israel) cites that anyone with ¼ Jewish blood (at least one grandparent who is Jewish) is considered Jewish and can come home and receive citizenship in Israel. This is a redemption of the horrible Nuremburg Laws which used the same measure of ¼ Jewish blood to condemn Jews to the Nazi Holocaust camps in the 1930's and 40's in Europe.

Rabbi Yaacov Kleinman[14] says of the "lost tribes,"

> Today's lost tribes of *Israel* are not in Afghanistan or the Far East; they are the Jews getting lost in the suburbs, in the universities, and in the corporate chase. A movement of spiritual return to Jewish roots and values is needed to help prevent these Jews and their descendants from becoming lost from the Tribe.

I heartily agree and pray for a spiritual return from lost-ness. I also believe that these groups rediscovering or discovering for the first time their Jewish heritage are a "first fruits" or a "down payment" for those who will come later who will fulfill literally the 144,000 from all the tribes of the Children of Israel. Which brings us to the large view of the "lost tribes."

חא

LARGE VIEW OF THE TEN LOST TRIBES*

THE SIZE OF 10-ISRAEL

The Torah records God's promise that even though the Land of Israel is being given to the Israelites, the tribes would be scattered to the four corners of the earth. This is God speaking to Jacob:

> **Genesis 28:14** Also your descendants shall be as the dust of the earth; you shall spread abroad to the west and the east, to the north and the south; and in you and in your seed all the families of the earth shall be blessed.

The previous scripture is nearly identical to God's promise to Abraham in

---

* The bulk of this Large View information comes from the historian Steven M. Collins who has authored five books on the tribes of Israel. Though I verified his sources, scriptural references and added my own insights, credit to his extensive work on this topic deserves more than an end note. Visit his website at stevenmcollins.com

> **Genesis 22:17-18** Blessing I will bless you, and multiplying I will multiply your descendants as the stars of the heaven and as the sand which *is* on the seashore; and your descendants shall possess the gate of their enemies. In your seed all the nations of the earth shall be blessed, because you have obeyed My voice."

Historically Christians have looked at the last phrase of these prophetic verses and said, "Oh look, there's Jesus. He is the Seed of Abraham that blesses all the families of the earth." While that is definitely true, there are other aspects of this prophecy that Christians have run over to get to the Jesus part. It is in this prophecy that we find an explanation of how the Hebrews multiply so rapidly, from God's phrasing of, "your descendants shall be as the dust of the earth."

Have you noticed the huge casualty numbers recorded in scripture?
- **Numbers 25:9** 24,000 people of Israel died by a plague of God
- **Judges 20:21-48** Battle of Retribution against Benjamin: 22,000 Israelites were killed on day one; 18,000 Israelites more on day two; 25,100 Benjamites plus 18,000 men of valor from Benjamin fell on day three.
- **1 Samuel 4:2** 4,000 men killed by Philistines in Battle of Aphek
- **2 Chronicles 28:6** 120,000 men killed in one day

Throughout the ages as Satan has tried to destroy the Jewish people, he has attempted great slaughters: 100,000 in Spain in the 1490's; 100-200,000 in the Ukraine in the 1640's; a minimum of 50,000 in the Russian Pogroms;[1] and 6,000,000 in the Nazi Holocaust. Even with a burgeoning earth population, because so many Jews have been wiped out throughout history, even the law of exponents doesn't seem to cover the birthrate of the chosen people adequately.

Birthrate

In four generations, Abraham, Isaac and Jacob, and his 12 sons, the Hebrews went from two people to 72 people. The 72 does not count the "other" sons of Abraham (Ishmael, the sons of Katurah, etc.) or Esau and his sons, all of whom broke away from this family line to live separately.

When these 72 moved to Egypt and lived there 400 years, they left Egypt as 603,550 (Numbers 1:44-47) fighting age men, not counting any Levites (22,000 men) nor women and children (unknown numbers). That is huge!

The multiplication factor is so high because of God's blessing: "your descendants shall be as the dust of the earth," "the stars of the heavens," and the "sand which is on the seashore."

The small view of the ten lost tribes popping up in these tiny numbers such as 800 here or 5,000 there as being the tribe of Manasseh or Levi does not factor in this standard of blessing that God cast over His chosen people. So while it is a start, I cannot see these small numbers as fulfillment, even if eventually a few people show up correctly claiming heritage from each distinct tribe. So let's dig deeper into some interesting big-picture anomalies in history. And while we dig, remember that what we accept as true history is always tainted by the worldview perspective of the one who wrote it (i.e. the "winners" write the history books.) and that Satan has an agenda to wipe away any trace of the God of Israel being real.

Assyrian Invasion
Our historical idea of "lost tribes" comes from the Ancient Assyrians sweeping into the Northern Kingdom as recorded in 2 Kings 17. Israelites from the 10 northern tribes were scattered abroad among the Assyrian lands in exile, and other peoples that the Assyrians had conquered were resettled in Israel.[15] The siege according to 2 Kings 17:5 lasted three years, and it wasn't really a surprise in its coming. The king of 10-Israel had been paying tribute money for years to stave off an attack. However, the only city listed as being besieged is Samaria. The Bible doesn't record that any of the rest of 10-Israel gave resistance to the Assyrians. As you read further, 2 Kings 17:24-26 describes a land that is inhabited by wild beasts, lions specifically. Biblical sources indicate and Assyrian records confirm that only about 27,000 Hebrews

were carried away captive to the cities of the Medes.[17] A remnant of the poor did get to remain in the land, but no Levites were among them, as indicated by the record in II Kings 17:24-28 when a Levitical priest was imported back to Israel to deal with the lion attacks sent by God because the new settlers were not worshipping Him properly.

Over 200 years before the Assyrians invaded, King David's census (2 Samuel 24:9) includes 800,000 "valiant men who drew the sword" living in Israel (plus 500,000 in Judah). That indicates a couple of million Israelites are occupying this territory, when the women, children, elderly and infirm people of Israel are included. But only 27,000 were carried away captive. So where did the rest go?

PHOENICIA

Let's backtrack a moment, first to some history you may not have studied in school. Phoenicia had its origins around 2800 BC and continued until it bowed to the Greek Empire in 332 lead by Alexander the Great.[27] However, the Phoenician Empire was not a single entity as we tend to think of an empire today, one with a single seat of governing power. "The Phoenician Empire from about 1000 to 700 BC was in fact the Israelite Empire, which was built under King David and King Solomon allied with King Hiram of Tyre and the other cities of Sidon and Byblos...that are commonly called Phoenician."[17] Even the Bible notes that these nations were intermingled and merged together. Solomon had many people coming down from Tyre to work on the Temple. Solomon drafted 30,000 Israelites to go north to work in groups of 10,000/month, besides the 153,000 foreigners living among them from which he assigned 70,000 burden bearers and 80,000 who quarried stone and 3,300 supervisors (1 Kings 5:13-15). Solomon and Hiram comingled their work crews (5:18) and navies (5:9). The famous mariners of Tyre and Sidon shared their special navigation skills with the Israelites.[17]

According to the Greeks, Homer and others, Phoenicia included a lot more than the coast of Lebanon (Tyre, Sidon, Byblos); the term *Phoenician* was used to refer to the whole east coast of the Mediterranean Sea.[17] The Phoenician Empire included colonies on the west coast of Europe and Africa and even into the British Isles, (called the "Tin Islands"[27]), at least. Some historians even speculate that the Phoenicians, as great seafarers, sailed around Africa to the West Indies in their trade.[27] However, the Phoenicians were only a world power from about 1000 BC to 700 BC, which exactly corresponds to the Golden Age of Israel (one nation) under Kings David and Solomon and then the split to two nations until Assyria conquered 10-Israel, then Phoenicia lost its influence and power. Even Wikipedia calls Phoenicia an, "ancient Semitic civilization situated on the western, coastal...Fertile Crescent and centered on the coastline of modern Lebanon...some colonies reaching the Western Mediterranean. It was an enterprising maritime trading culture that spread across the Mediterranean..."[26]

> **Not in your history book?** So why isn't this recorded in our history books—are you ready for a conspiracy theory? The god of this world doesn't want the truth to get out to the masses, so he colludes with governments and "leading scientists" to hide it, to laugh it off as a hoax, to ridicule believers of this data because instead of propagating their Evolutionary Theory which excludes a God who is coming again and Whose promises are true, these items point to not only a living God, but to a people who came before us who were intelligent enough to navigate the oceans often, not stupid Neanderthals who had not yet evolved to our level of intelligence.

Many Phoenician colony names contained or added the term BRT or BRTH. BRTH is a Hebrew word, pronounced *Bereth*. It means "Covenant." These Phoenician colony names show that they were made up of the covenant people.[17] This doesn't mean the Phoenicians *were* the covenant people, the Israelites are. "The fact that BRT was a dominant thread that ran through their alliance shows that the covenant people were proclaiming who they were among those peoples making up the Phoenicians. Phoenicia had a colony in Britain that included that BRT designator from about 1100 BC or before."[17] Another Phoenician colony was Carthage who had "BRT" imprinted on their coins. I Kings describes the international quality of Solomon's Empire.

> **I Kings 10:23-24** So King Solomon surpassed all the kings of the earth in riches and wisdom. 24 Now all the earth sought the presence of Solomon to hear his wisdom, which God had put in his heart.

Evidence found in North America indicates that the Phoenician Empire came to North America. (Forget everything you read in modern history books about Columbus discovering America!) They even had a large 20 acre temple to Ba'al in New Hampshire called Mystery Hill.[17] It's not as secret as you might think either. It is called "America's Stonehenge" on A&E's *America Unearthed* episode 6 which aired January 25, 2013.[21] Basements are all that remain because when American colonists came to New England they needed material to build their homes and towns, so they deconstructed the complexes they found and built cobblestone streets out of these bricks. Barry Fell of the Epigraphic Society found ancient inscriptions in Mystery Hill written in Phoenician, Carthaginian and Celtic languages. Mr. Fell and his crew crawled along streets and buildings with magnifying glasses and found inscriptions of the pagan gods mentioned in the Bible: Ba'al and Ashtoreth. Also preserved in the Eastern California Museum are stone inscriptions on a wall in Kufic (a derivative of Arabic). "The wall appeared to have been worked and reworked several times. Even the reworked portions showed signs of weathering and long exposure. The antiquity is simply undeniable."[19] All this evidence points to a Phoenician presence in North America!

NEW WORLD ROSETTA STONE

In Davenport, Iowa a New World equivalent of a Rosetta Stone was dug up in 1877, called the Davenport Stele. "According to Fell, the Davenport Stele contains a "trilingual text" in the Egyptian, Iberian-Punic, and Libyan languages. 'This stele, long condemned as a meaningless forgery, is in fact one of the most important steles ever discovered,' wrote Fell."[20] *Lybian* is not referring to the present-day country of Lybia, but the sea-fearing peoples of the Epyptians.[17] The Iberian-Punic language is a descendant language of Hebrew![17]

OHIO TEN COMMANDMENTS

The Ten Commandments were found on an ancient stone tablet in Ohio. The tablet was found in a casket containing a skeleton which crumbled when exposed to the air in one of the mounds along the Ohio River Valley in 1860. The engraving written in Hebrew showed that the hill was a Semitic grave.[22] But how did a Hebrew grave dating to such ancient times get into Ohio? Because they came over as part of the Phoenician Empire around the time of the scattering of the 10 Tribes. Even the Smithsonian Institute—after they turned the document right-side-up—ha!—very quietly asserts the connection between the Phoenician language and Ancient Hebrew block letters, found both in Israel and in Ohio.[23]

NEW MEXICO TEN COMMANDMENTS

The Ten Commandments were found on a large stone among other Hebrew writings in New Mexico! There is an inscription saying "Yahweh is our God"[17] in Paleo-Hebrew, the written language which was used from about 1200 BC.

Britain had been a Phoenician/Israelite Colony for about 300 years when Samaria fell to the Assyrians in 722 BC. The early Welch actually called themselves the Beryths related to Briton (Do you see the BRT/BRTH in Beryth?) meaning "covenant" in Hebrew.[24] Some people from the tribe of Dan were in this area. But most of 10-Israel emigrating from the Assyrians did not go that far. Many went to Carthage.[17] But most settled into a new home in the Black Sea Region.[17] (Evidence to follow in next chapters).

WERE THEY LOST?

The Jewish historian Josephus who wrote around the time of the sacking of Jerusalem and the Diaspora (70-72 AD) and from whom much of the history surrounding this time period is derived, did not think that 10-Israel was lost! In his book *Antiquities of the Jews* he writes, "(W)herefore there are but two tribes in Asia and Europe subject to the Iomans (Romans), while the ten tribes are beyond Euphrates (River) till now, and are an immense multitude, and not to be estimated by numbers."[18] Only 30 years after Jesus' death and resurrection, already God's Word about the sands of the sea and stars of the heaven is coming to pass!

Hosea prophesies that after God sends the Hebrews into captivity, that God would multiply them into an innumerable number.

> **Hosea 1:10-11** "Yet the number of the children of Israel Shall be as the sand of the sea, which cannot be measured or numbered. And it shall come to pass In the place where it was said to them, 'You *are* not My people,' *There* it shall be said to them, '*You are* sons of the living God.'[11] Then the children of Judah and the children of Israel shall be gathered together, And appoint for themselves one head; And they shall come up out of the land, for great *will be* the day of Jezreel!

Josephus already knew by his time, 800 years after 10-Israel's dispersion, that this prophecy had been fulfilled. The 10 tribes were not lost. Josephus and most of the first century world knew exactly where they were: the other side of the Euphrates.

Also in the first century, James was not confused about ten tribes being missing from 10-Israel. His book opens with "James, a bondservant of God and of the Lord Jesus Christ, To the twelve tribes which are scattered abroad: Greetings" (James 1:1). He was writing to all twelve tribes, not just Judah composed of two to three tribes.

תא

BIBLICAL CLUES TO FIND THE "LOST" TRIBES[25]

Even though Josephus and James and the general population of the first century were not confused, we obviously don't have this information readily available anymore, so in our search there are a few questions or clues we should be looking for when we go rummaging around history to find 10-Israel. According to

> **Jeremiah 51:5** "For Israel is not forsaken, nor Judah, By his God, the LORD of hosts, Though their land was filled with sin against the Holy One of Israel."

God has not and will not forsake Israel or Judah, no matter what the mainstream Western Christian Church has believed. (Notice also that God is referring to Israel and Judah as separate entities here). So what should we be searching for?

1. We should look for large group(s) of people.

Because of the Hosea 1:9-10 prophecy about the high number of people <u>after</u> their exile, and because Genesis 48:19 records a prophecy that Ephraim will become "the fullness of the nations." The fullness of nations sounds pretty huge to me.

2. We should look for migrating peoples and nations called by derivatives of the names Abraham and Isaac. (i.e. Brahman, Saka)

Genesis 21:12 says "in Isaac your seed is called" and Genesis 48:15-16 applies the name *Isaac* to Joseph's two sons Manasseh and Ephraim.

> [15] And he (Israel) blessed Joseph, and said:
> "God, before whom my fathers Abraham and Isaac walked, The God who has fed me all my life long to this day, [16] The Angel who has redeemed me from all evil, Bless the lads; Let my name be named upon them, And the name of my fathers Abraham and Isaac; And let them grow into a multitude in the midst of the earth."

3. We should look for a people who conquered the Neo-Assyrian Empire or hosted 10-Israel while Assyria was being conquered by them.

Isaiah 14:2b says "they will take them captive whose captives they were, and rule over their oppressors." Interestingly, the alliance of the Scythians, Cimmerians and Medes routed the Assyrians as far as Egypt between 627-605 BC. Note how "Scythians' is a derivative of Isaac and "Cimmerians" sounds just like Samarians, the same name as the capital city of 10-Israel which was besieged for three years by the Assyrians until 722 BC. The Assyrians had deported some of the 27,000 captive 10-Israelites to the region of the Medes. "Eventually much of Assyria's former lands would be ruled by the Parthian Empire (of Scythian/Saka stock) for nearly 500 years. Its first king was crowned in the city of *Assak* (Note the similarity in sound to "Isaak") in 247 BC"[25]

4. We should look for people(s) who migrate out of the Mede-Persian Empire and people(s) who were "afar off" during Daniel's time.

> **Daniel 9:7b** Prophecy: "...to the men of Judah, to the inhabitants of Jerusalem and <u>all Israel, those near and those far off</u> in all the countries to which You have driven them, because of the unfaithfulness which they have committed against You."

This seems to indicate that Daniel knew that some of Israel was near and some far off.

5. We should look for a diverse population, with "many colors," many cultures and traditions not one particular color or race.

   Genesis 37:3 "Now Israel loved Joseph more than all his children, because he *was* the son of his old age. Also he made him a tunic of *many* colors.

Everything means something in the scripture. Joseph was the one who received the coat. Joseph's sons were Ephraim and Manasseh. Even in their first generation they were not of "pure Israelite blood" because their mother was Egyptian.

6. We should not look for specific Jewish traditions and customs, or following Torah law.

Remember the reason 10-Israel was being exiled in the first place was because they were being disobedient and worshiping other gods. (See Daniel 9:7, p.46). Therefore it stands to reason that when they emigrated (left on their own) or were taken away captive, Jewish tradition and customs would not have been part of their culture. It would not have been a priority for them to carry Torah scrolls with them for instruction down the line. They would have clung to their idolatrous pagan ways and false gods.

7. We can identify 10-Israel by the nations who host Judah (the exiled and identifiable Jews) in the Last Days.

The following scriptures both indicate that in the last days Judah and 10-Israel will be walking together as they come out of exile back "home to Zion" out of Mystery Babylon.

   Jeremiah 3:17-18 "At that time Jerusalem shall be called The Throne of the LORD, and all the nations shall be gathered to it, to the name of the LORD, to Jerusalem. No more shall they follow the dictates of their evil hearts. 18 "In those days the <u>house of Judah shall walk with the house of Israel, and they shall come together out of the land of the north</u> to the land that I have given as an inheritance to your fathers.

Jeremiah 50:4-5 ""In those days and in that time," says the LORD, "The <u>children of Israel</u> shall come, They <u>and the children of Judah together;</u> With continual weeping they shall come, And seek the LORD their God.
⁵ They shall ask the way to Zion, With their faces toward it, *saying,* 'Come and let us join ourselves to the LORD *In* a perpetual covenant *That* will not be forgotten.'

8. We should look for people who currently (or historically) possess the "gate" of their enemy.

The "gate" refers to ways to get into and out of a nation or empire, such as narrow but significant sea channels, control of major ports, or major trade routes.

Genesis 24:60 prophecy/blessing: And they blessed Rebekah and said to her: "Our sister, *may* you *become The mother of* thousands of ten thousands; And may your <u>descendants possess The gates of those who hate them</u>."

CONCLUSION

These few clues may send your mind orbiting over the possibilities, once any minimalistic parameters have been removed and actual scriptural promises and clues are presented together. The following chapters will search for each tribe based on the prophetic blessing of Jacob recorded in Genesis 49 and from Moses in Deuteronomy 33.

3

IDENTIFYING 10-ISRAEL PART A

(SAGAS AND PEOPLES YOUR HISTORY BOOKS "FORGOT" TO MENTION)

A SNAPSHOT OF SCHOOL-BOOK HISTORY

US history books tend to start with civilization at the Sumerians in Asia Minor, and cover a little of Egypt as a side note. Then they usually remain focused on Asia Minor and the change of hands to the Babylonians and Assyrians and back to Babylonians as the major world power. With this focus it is as if the rest of the world's population doesn't exist. By the time of the Babylonians' second rise to power there is usually a mention of people gaining strength and influence in Greece and an acknowledgement that there are Egyptian and Israelite civilizations running concurrently, however they are only mentioned as opponents to the Asia Minor powers.

Usually the Phoenicians are given a light mention as ancient explorers in ships, but they are not presented as any rival empire with advanced technology or relevancy compared to Assyria or Babylon, nor are the Phoenicians' backgrounds discussed. Where did they come from? They are almost a footnote mentioned after the fact as a reason there are already people populating the Mediterranean when Asia Minor folks and Greek folks clash and go out migrating from the Caspian and Black Seas areas.

Then Rome takes a forefront in world history as they win the Punic Wars and conquer much of Asia and Europe. The people in the conquered areas make their way across Europe and seem to pop up out of nowhere in waves. The Greeks and Romans writing the history call them Visigoths, Gauls, Franks, Celts, Germanic Tribes, Saxons, Normans. And their records name this migration "The Barbarian Invasion," [92] explaining that it took place over several hundred years beginning around 300 BC.

Moving forward to the 600-1000's AD, usually our history books give a brief mention of the Byzantine Empire and the invasion of Islam, but focus predominantly on the expansion of Europe and integration of the "barbarians" to civilized life, including the Viking explorers, as they began to form nation states of Europe.[93]

There is not a lot of movement again until the "New World" is discovered, or rediscovered or something, because there are already people there. Then the books have to go back and describe how all the earth's land used to be glued together and that's how native people got to America.

Then England takes world dominance and her population sets out over the globe, only now we call it colonialism instead of conquering. America becomes the first to fully shake off England's rule and more migration from Europe takes place in the USA. Then some study is given to Modern Europe, but mostly our books focus on US History and wars, until WWI and II widen history to a more global scale again and we accept western Europe as an equal to us as we reshape the map lines in the Middle east (formerly Asia Minor/Byzantium/Ottoman Empire) and in eastern Europe. Sometimes it even gets mentioned that in 1948 a little state in the center of it all is formed for those Jews who've been wandering the planet for 2,000 years, taking advantage of countries kind enough to host them in their strange ways and superior, arrogant only-way God.

Snapshot of History Related to the Children of Abraham, Isaac and Jacob

King David and King Solomon created a wonderful place in the crossroads of the world economy for God's chosen people. There were easy alliances and integration with world super powers (Phoenician Empire) all along the Mediterranean Sea coast from (what we now call) the British Isles and Spain to Turkey and Lebanon, parts of Egypt and the north of Africa, Ethiopia and Libya. Most of these kingdoms shared information and technology with each other. After King Solomon's reign ended in 922 BC, Israel divided into the Kingdom of Judah and Kingdom of (10-) Israel. Each kingdom continued on under their own kings, with the dynasty of David ruling in Judah for 335 years (until 586 BC), and various family lines and usurpers ruling in 10-Israel for 201 years (until 721 BC).

Those last years in 10-Israel were not happy ones. Idol worship and sacrificing children by fire to false gods was rampant. The leadership was forceful and cruel, and many families immigrated to other areas within the Phoenician Empire. There is evidence of People of the Covenant living in Alexandria, in Spain, and even in the British Isles. Some families moved east and south to a separate empire called Parthia. As things got worse in 10-Israel and the Assyrians began to taunt them with takeover, many more families began to emigrate northward into present-day Carthage, Turkey and the Black Sea region. A few families, mostly Levites, even joined with their brothers in Judah to the south.

It was right at this time that a new empire is recorded as "coming out of no where," the Scythians. Scythia was located north of the Black Sea, in present day Romania, Ukraine, Russia, Georgia and Armenia. There is very interesting evidence—even in their name—of the Scythians as being the "Saka" or "Sacae" who were descended from Isaac/Isaak. While these people did not, for the most part, identify with their tribal names, they maintained their identity as a whole as those who descended from Isaak.[37]

From Scythia, groups of families migrated more and more westward, even as far as the Americas. These migratory people were probably referred to in your history books as the Anglos, the Saxons, the Goths, the Prussians, the Celts, the Gauls, and the Vikings etc. But I bet your history teacher never made the connection between these groups coming in to explore and settle inland Europe with the fall of the Scythian and Parthian Empires in the East happening at the exact same time.

The problem with our history is that it is predominately taken from one source: the Greco-Romans when they began to conquer the world.[1] They were full of pride in their accomplishments and seemed to think there was no intelligent life on earth until they arrived. While they did have a knack for engineering, their knowledge of geography and the earth left a lot to be desired. For centuries while Carthage was a dominant force in the Mediterranean, the Romans and Greeks were not allowed to enter the Atlantic Ocean.[84] Because Carthage was stronger than the Greeks and Romans, they even dictated where in the Mediterranean the Greeks and Romans could sail. Only after Rome won the Punic Wars in 146 BC were they able to control the Straight of Gibraltar and sail outside of it.[84]

In recording history according to the Greco-Roman worldview, they renamed people groups and former empires, if they bothered to mention them at all. There were great wars that the Greeks or Romans fought and lost against these great eastern empires, and yet because in the end the Romans won, there is hardly a mention of it in our records. For example, the Phoenicians did not call themselves by that name. It was assigned by the Greeks, way after the fact. "Carthage" was also a re-name in the Roman record books of a city that was actually called by the name "Kirjath Hadeshath" which is a Hebrew name meaning "new city."[1] 10-Israel continued to spread far and wide across the globe, usually attaching themselves to host countries, assimilating and blending in so that even they themselves forgot who they were by the 17th and 18th century AD, thus becoming the Ten Lost Tribes. However, by looking at specific traits and great migration movements, 10-Israel can be identified, if we are looking through the right lens of history (which always starts with the Word of God!).

תא

JACOB'S BLESSING IN GENESIS 49.

This is a bit long, but really read it, because it provides the clues we will be following to find 10-Israel among us today. In the NKJV this chapter is titled "Jacob's last words to his sons." It even starts in the very first verse with the bold statement that this prophetic statement is what will happen to the sons of Israel in the *last days*. It doesn't get any more obvious a clue than that! I don't think anyone would argue that we are currently living in the last days.

> **Genesis 49:1-28** And Jacob called his sons and said, "Gather together, <u>that I may tell you what shall befall you in the last days</u>: ² "Gather together and hear, you sons of Jacob, And listen to Israel your father. ³"Reuben, you are my firstborn, My might and the beginning of my strength, The excellency of dignity and the excellency of power. ⁴ Unstable as water, you shall not excel, Because you went up to your father's bed; Then you defiled *it*—He went up to my couch.
>
> ⁵ "Simeon and Levi *are* brothers; Instruments of cruelty *are in* their dwelling place. ⁶ Let not my soul enter their council; Let not my honor be united to their assembly; For in their anger they slew a man, And in their self-will they hamstrung an ox. ⁷ Cursed *be* their anger, for *it is* fierce; And their wrath, for it is cruel! I will divide them in Jacob And scatter them in Israel.
>
> ⁸ "Judah, you *are he* whom your brothers shall praise; Your hand *shall be* on the neck of your enemies; Your father's children shall bow down before you. ⁹ Judah *is* a lion's whelp; From the prey, my son, you have gone up.

He bows down, he lies down as a lion; And as a lion, who shall rouse him? ¹⁰ The scepter shall not depart from Judah, Nor a lawgiver from between his feet, Until Shiloh comes; And to Him *shall be* the obedience of the people. ¹¹ Binding his donkey to the vine, And his donkey's colt to the choice vine, He washed his garments in wine, And his clothes in the blood of grapes.

¹² His eyes *are* darker than wine, And his teeth whiter than milk. ¹³ "Zebulun shall dwell by the haven of the sea; He *shall become* a haven for ships, And his border shall adjoin Sidon. ¹⁴ "Issachar is a strong donkey, Lying down between two burdens; ¹⁵ He saw that rest *was* good, And that the land *was* pleasant; He bowed his shoulder to bear *a burden,* And became a band of slaves. ¹⁶ "Dan shall judge his people As one of the tribes of Israel. ¹⁷ Dan shall be a serpent by the way, A viper by the path, That bites the horse's heels So that its rider shall fall backward. ¹⁸ I have waited for your salvation, O LORD!
¹⁹ "Gad, a troop shall tramp upon him, But he shall triumph at last. ²⁰"Bread from Asher *shall be* rich, And he shall yield royal dainties. ²¹"Naphtali *is* a deer let loose; He uses beautiful words.
²² "Joseph *is* a fruitful bough, A fruitful bough by a well; His branches run over the wall. ²³ The archers have bitterly grieved him, Shot *at him* and hated him.
²⁴ But his bow remained in strength, And the arms of his hands were made strong By the hands of the Mighty *God* of Jacob (From there *is* the Shepherd, the Stone of Israel),
²⁵ By the God of your father who will help you, And by the Almighty who will bless you *With* blessings of heaven above, Blessings of the deep that lies beneath, Blessings of the breasts and of the womb. ²⁶ The blessings of your father Have excelled the blessings of my ancestors, Up to the utmost bound of the everlasting hills. They shall be on the head of Joseph, And on the crown of the head of him who was separate from his brothers.
²⁷ "Benjamin is a ravenous wolf; In the morning he shall devour the prey, And at night he shall divide the spoil."

²⁸ All these *are* the twelve tribes of Israel, and this *is* what their father spoke to them. And he blessed them; he blessed each one according to his own blessing.

JOSEPH AND THE BIRTHRIGHT

In the scripture above, Joseph receives the attention of only two verses, 22-23, but the entire previous chapter (Genesis 48) is devoted to Joseph's two sons' blessing and inheritance, which appears to have been bestowed in a separate, perhaps earlier, blessing ceremony. Joseph, eldest son of Jacob's beloved wife Rachel received the birthright over all of his brothers. We will cover the detail of that in a coming chapter, but for now it is important to note that the inheritance birthright was passed from Abraham to Isaac in Genesis 25:5 which says, "Abraham gave all that he had to Isaac." This inheritance included all the promises of God laid out in the covenant of Genesis 15. The Covenant included God's protection (Gen 15:1), great numbers of offspring (Gen 15:5), and the land of Israel (Gen 15:7). God reiterated his promise as recorded in Genesis 17. This inheritance was then passed from Isaac to Jacob in full, since he received both the inheritance (as traded for a bowl of stew in Genesis 25:33) and his father's blessing below.

> **Genesis 27: 28-29** Therefore may God give you
> Of the dew of heaven,
> Of the fatness of the earth,
> And plenty of grain and wine.
> ²⁹ Let peoples serve you,
> And nations bow down to you.
> Be master over your brethren,
> And let your mother's sons bow down to you.
> Cursed *be* everyone who curses you,
> And blessed *be* those who bless you!"

So Jacob received rains, wealth, servants, international leadership and favor and God's blessing or curse over other nations based on their interactions with Jacob, in addition to the land, the great numbers of offspring and God's protection.

When Jacob passed an inheritance and blessing on to his 12 sons, there was a change in protocol. For the first time the inheritance was not fully intact, but broken up among the brothers, and the birthright was a double portion of the inheritance. Jacob/Israel said it like this, "Moreover I have given to you one portion above your brothers, which I took from the hand of the Amorite with my sword and my bow" (Genesis 48:22).

At the time of the birthright blessing, Joseph and his two sons, Manasseh and Ephraim, were called to receive it. Because the two sons were blessed with the birthright double portion it immediately became a blessing that had been quadrupled. This quad-share of the inheritance for Ephraim and Manasseh only inconvenienced the other sons/tribes when they were dividing up the Promised Land. The other blessings were intangible, though still just as real; Ephraim and Manasseh received a double portion of God's protection, riches, international favor and high birthrate. We will see this demonstrated in the following chapters when we find Ephraim and Manasseh among the modern nations.

תא

First Issue of Disappearance begins with Tribe of Simeon

Long before there was even a Kingdom of Israel to split, there was a problem with many missing Simeonites. The two censuses taken in the desert about 40 years apart prove this. Numbers 1:22 records the Simeonite fighting age men who came out of Egypt as numbering 59,300. Forty years later Numbers 26:14 records Simeon's population at 22,200. That is more than half their population which is missing! They went from being the third largest tribe to the smallest. While some tribe populations went up and others went down there was only a total difference of 1,820 people over those 40 years.

Tribe of	1st count	2nd count	difference
Simeon	59,300	22,200	-37,100

So what happened between Numbers 1 and 26? Well, immediately before the second census, Numbers 25 records that harlotry was entering the Hebrew camp and that Israel had joined themselves to Baal Peor the god of Moab through the foreign women. The Lord's anger was aroused and He sent a plague into the camp. Phinehas (grandson of Aaron) stopped it by killing a man who was bold in his voracious sin, presenting his woman, a Midianite, to Moses in front of the weeping-in-their-sin Israelites.

Numbers 25:14-15 describes what this plague might have to do with the missing Simeonites:

> [14] Now <u>the name of the Israelite who was killed</u>, who was killed with the Midianite woman, <u>*was* Zimri the son of Salu, a leader of a father's house among the Simeonites.</u> [15] And the name of the Midianite woman who was killed *was* Cozbi the daughter of Zur; he *was* head of the people of a father's house in Midian.

The blatant offender who had to die was a Simeonite leader. The censuses difference of 37,100 fighting age men (plus their families) in Simeon's tribe cannot be explained away merely by saying that all 24,000 Hebrews who died in the plague of God came from this one Simeonite tribe. First, the number is not large enough, and second, the book of Numbers doesn't say that all 24,000 people were men of fighting age. If the plague deaths had been entirely among the tribe of Simeon, it would have been recorded as a plague against Simeon.

Simeon was a hothead, even from his youth, and this trait was passed on through his generations. Even to the end of days the Simeonites will be recognized by this trait. Jacob prophesied it over his son (see box). So it is not unreasonable to extrapolate that there could have been an unrecorded "walk-out" lead by the Simeonites who were mad that one of their leaders was killed in such a shameful manner.

> **GENESIS 49**
> **SIMEON PROPHECY**
> [5]"Simeon and Levi *are* brothers; Instruments of cruelty *are in* their dwelling place. [6] Let not my soul enter their council; Let not my honor be united to their assembly; For in their anger they slew a man, And in their self-will they hamstrung an ox.
> [7] Cursed *be* their anger, for *it is* fierce; And their wrath, for it is cruel! I will divide them in Jacob and scatter them in Israel.

Collins presents his theory,

> It is my belief that after the execution (of) a Simeonite prince by a Levitical priest, there was a great dissension in the camp of Israel. We know from the accounts in the Torah of their wanderings in the Wilderness that the Israelites were very prone to revolting against Moses over various provocations. We know from Genesis 34:25 that Simeon and Levi were the two most impulsive sons of Jacob, the two most likely to settle a matter 'by the sword.' To put it in modern American terms, they were the kind who 'shot first and asked questions later.' Genesis 49:5-7 prophesies that impulsive wrathfulness leading to violence would characterize both Simeonites and Levites through all the millennia up to and including the 'latter days'.[2(para8)]

From this dissention in Israel and its being resolved 37,100 Simeonites lighter, there had to have been some sort of walk out. This second "exodus" was probably led by the Simeonites, since they represented the greatest number of missing people, even counting regular demographic growth.[2] However there is another tribe which has a great reduction in their numbers too. It is Ephraim. Ephraim was a "birthright tribe" like Manasseh whose population burgeoned an extra 20,000 people in 40 years.

Ephraim should have walked in this same multiplication blessing of the "birthright," (Can we call it a birthright birthrate?) yet they are down by 8,000 instead of up by 25,000. That is quite a difference. If we were to take the fighting men who "disappeared" just from these two tribes, Simeon and Ephraim, and add their families to the total, we could quite possible have a group as large as 200,000 ex-Israelites looking to strike out on their own from the wilderness, years before coming into the Promised Land.[2] How much they are like Jacob's Genesis 49:7b statement, "I will divide them in Jacob and scatter them in Israel."

Tribe	1st count	2nd count	Difference
Manasseh	32,200	52,700	+20,500
Ephraim	40,500	32,500	-8,000

This mass walk-out could have even been the event that instigated the second census, as in "whose side will you be counted on?" If you question whether God would have allowed such a mass evacuation, think about God's nature. Does He ever force people to choose Him and His ways? No. Living with Him is always by invitation. If you say "no," He will let you go, but His hopeful eye will always be watchful for your slightest turn toward Him again.

It is quite obvious God didn't "lose" them when they "went missing." (And both of these tribes and all the other tribes were still highly represented among the 13 tribes of Israel.) But where did Simeon-Ephraim go? It was not a small group of wanderers, and one of the major representing tribes had the birthright birthrate to keep up high multiplication perpetually! Let's look at some ancient peoples that we do know about from our Greco-Roman history and see if we can find Simeonite characteristics among them.

SIMEONITE CLUES FROM HISTORICAL NATURE OF THE SPARTANS.[2] There are at least two groups that display Israelite characteristics:

1. The Sea People who raided and settled the Mediterranean World
2. The Spartans of Ancient Greece

I lean more toward the Spartans being the run-away Simeon-Ephraimites based on several items of historical and characteristic evidence: The Spartans claim to be descended from a people group who were non-native to Greece, but who arrived there in ancient times. The Spartans were famous for being very aggressive and warlike. It was they who held back the Persian Empire and Xerxes with a fighting force of just 300 elite Spartan bodyguards and 1,100 others in the Battle of Thermopylae in 480 BC.[4] Of all the Greek city-states the Spartans were most martial and even famous for it.[2] Based on Jacob's prophecy, Simeon would likely be full of men who would "live by the sword." The Spartans were known for being ruthless, and the Simeonites were known for being "instruments of cruelty," "angry" and "fierce" (Genesis 49:5-7).

A professor of Ancient History at Cambridge University, A.H.M. Hill, wrote *Sparta* in 1967 in which he describes the Spartans worshipping a great "lawgiver" in their "distant past."[3(p. 5)] Could it be Moses? Hill also writes that the Spartans observed monthly new moon celebrations and the "seventh day."[3] Both of these observations find their earthly origins in the Israelite culture.[3] Could the ancient Simeon-Ephraimite runaways who had spent 40 years basing their lives around the new moon and the Sabbath celebrations have decided to take that with them? Hill also describes that the ancient Spartans divided themselves up into smaller "tribes which constituted distinct military formations within the Spartan army."[3(p. 31-32)] This makes sense if they were originally from many of the formerly Israelite tribes. The Spartans founded a colony in Italy called Tara. Which is a Semitic/Hebrew name (spelled in English: Terah), after Abraham's father. Perhaps also, their forefather?[2]

The most profound evidence comes from a letter written by the Spartans themselves in which they call the Jews their "kinsmen" or "brethren" as the following version records in I Maccabees 14:16-23:

> This is a copy of the letter which the Spartans sent: "The rulers and the city of the Spartans to Simon the high priest and to the elders and the priests and the rest of the Jewish people, our brethren, greeting.

They were not claiming to *be* Jews, but rather Jewish *kinsmen*, as they would if they were from another tribe of Israel. Collins concludes his writing,

> That the Spartans acknowledged a common ancestry with the Jews of the tribe of Judah gives powerful weight to the assertion that they were Israelites who migrated to Greece instead of the Promised Land. The Spartan culture is most like that of the tribe of Simeon, most of which apparently left the Israelite encampment in the Wilderness after a Simeon(ite) prince was executed by a Levite.[2] (para 25)

So it is quite probable that the missing Simeonites are not missing at all, just grown to such a large population size (birthright birthrate), out from under the Lord's law, that they are difficult to recognize.

Sparta became prideful and was conquered by the Greeks, remaining a relatively minor state until the Romans conquered them in 146 BC, and they were absorbed into the population as their culture broke down.

THE 740-721 BC DISPERSION OF 10-ISRAEL

Life continued for the Israelites in the manner with which we are familiar from Biblical records until the Assyrians began to take over 10-Israel's territory in 720 BC (II Kings 17). God saved Judah from this same fate (for another 135 years) because they repented and humbled themselves before God, lead by King Hezekiah. This invasion came in waves over a 20 year period, which ended in a three year siege against Samaria. "At the beginning of this period, the Assyrians took captive the tribe of Naphtali and the Gileadite tribes of Gad, Reuben and the half tribe of Manasseh (II Kings 15:29)."[7](para 1) These groups were carried eastward into Asia. Many bright 10-Israel folks saw that the Assyrians kept coming back; they gathered their families and fled west to different Phoenician colonies around the Mediterranean Sea with which they were familiar because previous generations had spread there through the centuries as far back as the time of King David. These were the Phoenician colonies whose names contained the BRTH, the name of covenant, upon them (see chapter 2).

Some towns and families of 10-Israel went a different direction instead of being captured by Assyria. They went north and east.

A FEW THINGS TO REMEMBER AS WE GO SEARCHING FOR THESE ESCAPEES:

1. The people, even in their filthy sin and punishment, were still Israel, the chosen people, and sealed with an irrevocable blessing (even though God did withdraw His blessing from time to time, He always invoked it again).

2. Particularly Ephraim and Manasseh held the birthright double blessing (Genesis 48) which included the high birthrate, wealth, and national power.[7]

3. The Hosea 1:1-10 prophecy about 10-Israel being scattered and <u>then</u> being greatly increased in number.

4. The Genesis 21:12 prophecy that Israel will be known by Abraham's name and the name of his son, Isaak/Isaac.

5. The Genesis 48:14 prophecy that the tribes of Ephraim and Manasseh will bear the name of Isaac throughout history. Amos 7:16 shows that this was already happening before the exile when Amos refers to "the house of Israel" as the "house of Isaac."[7] "In ancient times, vowels were not written, so the consonants of Isaac's name would be "S-C" or "S-K" (dependent on the language in which the word appeared)."[7(para 5)] Jim Jester's article "Identifying Israel Part 4," confirms this ancient way of writing without the use of vowels, even though they were pronounced when speaking.[10(Scythian Domination para 2)] Even modern Hebrew only contains consonants, with an occasional vowel placeholder like the alef; so if

IDENTIFYING 10-ISRAEL PART A

you've ever seen the strange looking dots and dashes under Hebrew letters, you are looking at the vowel-pronunciation guide for beginning speakers.

6. When names are translated into other languages, or people conquer a place and then write down their version of history, they may spell names and places differently, but phonetically they usually sound quite similar. However when combining the lack of vowels problem of #5 and this change of ancient languages and then translation into English some almost unrecognizable changes have occurred.

LET'S SEARCH OUT THE HIDDEN TREASURES

Let's start by applying the Genesis 21:12 clue, so we should look for 10-Israel by searching for tribes which contain or add Isaac's name to their region and people. And Isaac's name was spelled in Hebrew sheen, kuf (SK or SC) and was pronounced EAT-sock. (Doesn't that sound delicious.)

Well, there happens to be a large group located around the Black Sea Region with the sound of Isaac's name attached to them…and they appeared in history at the exact time of 10-Israel's exile, in the 7th century BC![8] The Scythians. This group was also known as the *Sacae* or *Saka*. The names Sacae and Saka are interchangeable since the "ae" is the Latin form that pluralizes a noun, much the same function as our "s." So "Sacae" is the plural form of "Saka." And "Scythians" is the original Greek name for the same people group. Interestingly, this group of Scythians (Greek) or Sacae (Latin) fulfill all six of the above criteria. See the name of Isaac upon them in the SC or SK of his name?

As we delve into the details of names in order to "find" the 10 lost tribes, I have found it helpful to pronounce the ancient place and people names aloud to hear the phonetic linking in sound that is not readily identifiable in the written text. Using the example above, the name *Isaac* pronounced EAT-sock), and the people of Scythia were called SOCK-uh (the accent is on the all capital letters) or SOCK-a in plural. In saying it out loud, can you hear the sameness of how people of "EAT-sock" (Isaac) are called the "SOCK-a" (Saka)? In the spelling though, because the hard sound a K or C makes is identical, translating historians have used different spellings, and thus to the untrained eye, it looks like different people groups. The translator's accent in treating vowel sounds makes up the different spellings for the same words. If English speaking peoples did not have a standard spelling guide (i.e. a dictionary) we would have the same problem in spelling the same words.

EXAMPLES OF PRONUNCIATION

When saying the word *aluminum*, people in South Africa sound different from New Yorkers or people from Atlanta, Georgia, yet because we have agreed on how to spell it, we all know that we are referring to the same element.

Another example is Cimmerans and Sumarians. They look totally different, and if accented similarly to cinnamon, Cimmerans (Simer-ANS) sounds nothing like the way English speakers pronounce Sumarians (Suh-MARY-ins). But when we realize that the C and S are interchangeable in sound like in *circle (SER-kle)*, it is not a stretch to hear that *Cimmerans* and *Sumarians* are referring to the same people group.

תא

THE ANCIENT SCYTHIAN PEOPLE

The Scythians are a people who appear on the historical record in the 7th century BC. They settled in the present-day Crimea area, "the region covering parts of modern-day Crimea, Kazakhstan, Russia, Poland, the Ukraine valley, Belarus, Romania, and northern India."[6(para 1)] Most of the data we know about them comes from the Greek source, Herodotus. But Tamara Talbot Rice, a historian of the Scythian peoples wrote,

> The Scythians did not become a recognizable national entity… before the eighth century B.C…by the seventh century B.C. they had established themselves firmly in

southern Russia...Assyrian documents place their appearance...on the shores of Lake Urmia [just south of Armenia] in the time of King Sargon (722-705 B.C.) a date which closely corresponds with that of the first establishment of the first group of Scythians in southern Russia."[11]

It is important to note that while Judah received a prophetic 70-year sentence of exile, 10-Israel was given no promise of a specific date when they could expect to return. However, about 100 years after 10-Israel was gone from the land, the same prophet who voiced those 70 years for Judah, also sent a message from God to 10-Israel, Jeremiah 3 records this reconciliation message even as God proclaims Judah's demise.

> **Jeremiah 3:11-15** Then the LORD said to me (Jeremiah), "Backsliding Israel has shown herself more righteous than treacherous Judah. [12] Go and proclaim these words <u>toward the north</u>, and say:
> 'Return, backsliding Israel,' says the LORD; 'I will not cause My anger to fall on you. For I *am* merciful,' says the LORD; 'I will not remain angry forever. [13] Only acknowledge your iniquity, That you have transgressed against the LORD your God, And have scattered your charms To alien deities under every green tree, And you have not obeyed My voice,' says the LORD.
> [14] "Return, O backsliding children," says the LORD; "for I am married to you. I will take you, one from a city and two from a family, and I will bring you to Zion. [15] And I will give you shepherds according to My heart, who will feed you with knowledge and understanding.

Interesting isn't it, that God told Jeremiah to send the message *north* to 10-Israel. Again, 10-Israel was not lost to God. He knew exactly where to reach them. God told Jeremiah that they lived "to the north" of Jeremiah's location in Jerusalem. Drawing a line northward from Jerusalem we run into the Black Sea region, exactly where ancient sources place a large body of migrating Israelites. The people living in that region were known as "Scythians" or the "Sacae" tribes.[7]

MORE THAN COINCIDENCE. If just the name, location and time of appearance on the historical scene were all the information we had to link 10-Israel as being the Scythians, we might pass it off as coincidence, but there is more. Scythia did not remain rooted only in the north-from-Jerusalem Black Sea region; they spread eastward to the Steppes and Caucasus Mountains as their population expanded quickly.[7] (Birthright Birthrate, perhaps.) The capital city early in Scythian history was named "Sakiz."[7] Perhaps it was their wish to show a historical connection to their Patriarch, Isaac.

Two other historical accounts of the Scythians lend evidence to the Scythians/Sacae being 10-Israel. "The Greek story of Xenophon mentions the 'Sacians' of Asia who 'suffered very severely' at the hands of the Assyrians, and a Roman writer, Pliny, stated the Scythians were 'descended from slaves'."[7 (para 12)] Apparently, it's hard to shake a past of slavery. It had been 800-1,000 years since Israel had been slaves in Egypt.

HERODOTUS' RECORD OF SCYTHIA. Ancient historian Herodotus "noted the presence of 'Sacae' in both the army and navy of the Persian monarch, Xerxes,"[7(para 12)] around 480 BC. Another interesting tidbit recorded by Herodotus is, "They [the Scythians] make no offerings of pigs, nor will they keep them in their country."[7(para 12)] Since the Scythians would not keep pigs in their country nor use them for sacrifice, it stands to reason that they did not eat pork either. Could this be another link to a Torah-based past? Herodotus records an instance of a man, Anacharsis, being dragged before the Scythian king who personally executed the man for wearing idols and indulging in Greek religious ceremonies of worship which were not allowed in Scythia.[7] Incidentally, the king's name was Saulius, a derivative of the name Saul, the first king of Israel.[7]

"Although Herodotus wrote that the 'stupidest nations in the world' lived in the Black Sea region, he exempted the Scythians from this negative classification. The term 'Scythian' came to describe a lifestyle as much as a national ancestry."[7(para 14)]

After reading about the Scythians following a couple of the laws of Torah such as some dietary laws and not allowing idol worship, it is easier to understand God's statement to Jeremiah when He said, "Backsliding Israel has shown herself more righteous than treacherous Judah" (Jeremiah 3:11).

REGIONAL NAMES EVIDENCE. Originally some of the rivers that emptied into the Black Sea were called Ister, Tyras, Borysthenes and Tanais. When the Scythians moved in, they renamed those rivers to the names by which they are still called to this day: the Danube, the Dniester, the Dnieper and the Don. These are "Israelite names based on the name of the Israelite tribe of Dan…The Israelite tribe of Dan had a tendency to re-name geographical locations after its own tribal name."[7 (para 16)] Joshua records just such a renaming early in their history.

> **Joshua 19:47** And the border of the children of Dan went beyond these, because the children of Dan went up to fight against Leshem and took it; and they struck it with the edge of the sword, took possession of it, and dwelt in it. They called Leshem, Dan, after the name of Dan their father.

HEBREW NAMES EVIDENCE. The Scythians lived in the Black Sea region and Caucasus Mountains. Scythia had an ally relationship with a new kingdom named Iberia just before the time of Jesus in the first century. They were known as the Caucasian Iberians. The Kingdom of Iberia was ruled by a family of kings named "Pharesmenes."[7] The word "Iberia" comes from the name *Eber*, the great grandson of Shem (Genesis 11:10-26) and ancestor of Abraham from whom we derive the original name of the Israelites, "the Hebrews." Iber was written the same way Eber was (bet, resh or BR) because we know that the Semitic languages did not use written vowels, they were only pronounced.

Further evidence of this link between Eber and Hebrew is that when Eber or Iber is pluralized with the "im" it becomes Iberim. (We pronounce this name *Abram* in English). Iberim was the father of the Hebrews. The name Eber has been associated with Israel since Abraham, and this Iberian colony outpost in present-day Spain was likely established when Israel was sailing the Mediterranean and beyond during the reins of David and Solomon.

> This same name, "Iberia," had previously been placed upon the modern region of Spain and Portugal, which were formerly part of the Phoenician Empire of Israel, Tyre and Sidon. The name "Pharesmenes" includes the exact name of Phares, the ancestor of King David, to whom the promise of royal descendants was given.[7(para 17)]

DAVIDIC NAMES EVIDENCE: The Massagetae Tribe and Queen Tomyris.[7] About 528 BC, in the lifetime of Daniel, the Persians led by Cyrus the Great invaded the Scythian tribes who by this time had spread to the Caspian Sea. The principle ruling Scythian tribe's name was Massagetae and their queen was Tomyris. The name "Massa-getae" bears a striking similarity to the name of the leading Israelite tribe of Manasseh. Also, King David was promised in I Kings 8:25 that his progeny would perpetually include rulers over the people of Israel."[7(para 18)] The name of Queen Tomyris when broken into syllables (Tom-yr-is) bears a striking resemblance to the Hebrew name Tamar, a popular name in King David's lineage. (David's daughter, granddaughter and the mother of Pharez, David's ancestor all carried this name.) In fact when the vowels are removed (as usual in ancient spellings) from this queen's name the two names are identical, T-M-R.[7]

> The presence of names from King David's lineage among the Scythian tribes confirms that the Scythians were descended from the ten tribes of Israel, as God's promise indicated David's progeny would specifically rule over the ten tribes of Israel throughout history.[7(para 20)]

IDENTIFYING 10-ISRAEL PART A

A 10-ISRAEL/SCYTHIAN AND JUDAH STORY[10]

There is one more Bible story that makes sense when explained in light of part of 10-Israel being the Scythians. King Josiah reigned in Judah about 639-608 BC, (around 30 years before Judah would be exiled to Babylon). While Josiah was restoring the temple of God, 2 Chronicles 34:8-33 records that the high priest Hilkiah uncovered a Book of God's Law, and Josiah read it. Josiah was distraught to the point of weeping and tearing his clothes. He repented and read the Covenant to the people. They all begin to keep Passover (2 Chronicles 35). But an interesting, twice-mentioned phrase comes into play as the scripture records this Passover celebration King Josiah reinstituted in Judah:

> **2 Chronicles 35:17-19.** And the <u>children of Israel who were present</u> kept the Passover at that time, and the Feast of Unleavened Bread for seven days. [18] There had been no Passover kept <u>in Israel</u> like that since the days of Samuel the prophet; and none of the <u>kings of Israel</u> had kept such a Passover as Josiah kept, with the priests and the Levites, <u>all Judah and Israel who were present, and the inhabitants of Jerusalem</u>. [19] In the eighteenth year of the reign of Josiah this Passover was kept.

"The children of Israel" Wait?! *Israel* was present in *Judah*? What? When? Verse 19 gives us the exact year this occurred, "the 18th year of Josiah's reign." 10-Israel had been exiled and scattered for over a hundred years by this time. What were they doing there (besides celebrating Passover with their brothers!)? The Scripture doesn't tell us, but other historical sources do.

The Scythians were at war, conquering the present-day Middle East from their home near the Black Sea, as could be expected of angry warring tribes who had been compelled to leave their home territory three to five generations earlier. Herodotus records this campaign taking place around 620 BC. He even records the Scythians entering the Holy Land and staying for 10-25 years. The Scythians/Sacae completely ravaged the Assyrian territory. Why were they so harsh to Assyria? The Assyrians were the people who had conquered and killed their 10-Israel great-grandfather's brothers and families who didn't escape. The Scythians occupied the Black Sea region, Asia Minor, Syria, Media, much of Assyria, former-10-Israel, and as far south as the border of Egypt from around 624 BC.[10] However, they left Judea alone. Their occupation included 10-Israel area but they spared Judah's cities. The Scythians sparing tiny Judah would make no sense if the Scythians "were wild nomads from northern Asia who were in Palestine for the first time. However, it is completely logical when one realizes that as descendants of the ten tribes of Israel, the Scythians were blood relatives of the Jews"[10(para 15)]

Some Scythians remained in their ancient 10-Israel homeland for 10-25 years, but then the majority moved back to their cities in the north around the Black Sea and over into Russia due to overcrowding in their ancient Israelite homeland. Remember 10-Israel in exile still had the effect of the birthright birthrate propelling their population numbers upward in both Ephraim and Manasseh. This Scythian/10-Israel generation may have heard from their parents and grandparents about Israel's land of milk and honey. Perhaps they had heard stories of its glorious past under Kings David and Solomon, but it had been left in ruins and resettled by a few Assyrian captives from other lands. It was no joyful homecoming as they might have hoped.[10] So, after giving resettling a shot, they moved back to what *their* generation called "home."

So why doesn't the Scripture record the Scythian invasion? Because "Scythian" is the Greek name, just as Sacae was what they called themselves (after their ancestor Isaac, as was prophesied). But God and Judah referred to them as "children of Israel," because that is who they were: Israel coming home, not lost. And for at least that one Passover, maybe more during their 10-25 years back, Israel and Judah celebrated the Lord's Passover as one. That repentant Passover day of celebration was a foreshadow, a rehearsal, of the reunification that will occur at the end of the last days when Israel and Judah will no longer be separated, but will be one under God again!

SCYTHIANS TODAY

At the same time "the ten tribes of Israel 'disappeared' from their old territory, the Scythians (bearing the name of Isaac) 'appeared' near the Black Sea and spread throughout the Russian steppes. The connection between the Israelites and Sacae/Scythians is not hard to understand."[10(final para.)] **Sheldon Emry, author of *Heirs of the Promise*,** helps us connect what we have been taught by lack-luster Greco-Roman sources to this uncovered relationship of the Scythians to Israel.

> Our history books pick up the story at this point recording the westward migrations of the Scythians and their contact with the Cimmerians, who had earlier settled west of the Black Sea. Their kinship lost over the centuries and ensuing battles forced them westward to become the Celts, Gauls, and Cimbri. By the end of the fourth century B.C. the Scythians had established a great and prosperous kingdom.[9]

The ancient Scythians became the multiple waves of western immigration to Europe that today we call the Celts, Gauls and Cimbri.

תא

ABUNDANCE OF ASIAN JEWS

Just a small Biblical tidbit to verify the Jews being found in great numbers across the Asian continent: Remember the record of Esther? Although Esther descended from the tribe of Benjamin (Esther 2:5-7) in Judah and her family had been exiled after the 586 BC invasion of the Babylonians, not the 10-Israel exile 135 years earlier, many of the chosen people in the Babylonian Empire where Esther ruled as queen "for such as time as this" were from 10-Israel.

When Haman's plot to annihilate the Jews was exposed and undone by Mordecai, the announcement went all over the continent because the Jews were living all over the Persian Empire.

> **Esther 8:9b** and it was written, according to all that Mordecai commanded, to the Jews, the satraps, the governors, and the princes of the provinces <u>from India to Ethiopia, one hundred and twenty-seven provinces</u> *in all*, to every province in its own script, to every people in their own language, and to the Jews in their own script and language.

This is evidence of more fulfilled prophecy: that 10-Israel would be more prolific after their exile than before. They were everywhere in Asia, even after the kingdom of Judah began making her way back after the prescribed 70 years were fulfilled.

When speaking of Esther's record, it is important also to mention Esther 8:17 where, after the King's decree went out and the Jews were allowed to defend themselves, it became popular to be Jewish, so that "many people of the land became Jews."(NKJV) The people of Persia were a mixed group from all the lands the Persians had conquered, including Israelites (of 10-Israel) who had been conquered by the Assyrians who had been conquered by the Babylonians and then the Medes, and also people of Judah who had decided not to return home after the 70 years were up (90%).

To "become Jewish" was a provision God made for Gentiles in the Torah (Leviticus 9:33-34) for those who were not born as sons of Abraham but want to join themselves to the God of Israel. It is also feasible that some of those mentioned as "becoming Jewish" may have been former 10-Israelites or Judahites who were rededicating themselves to the Covenant and God.

Identifying 10-Israel Part B

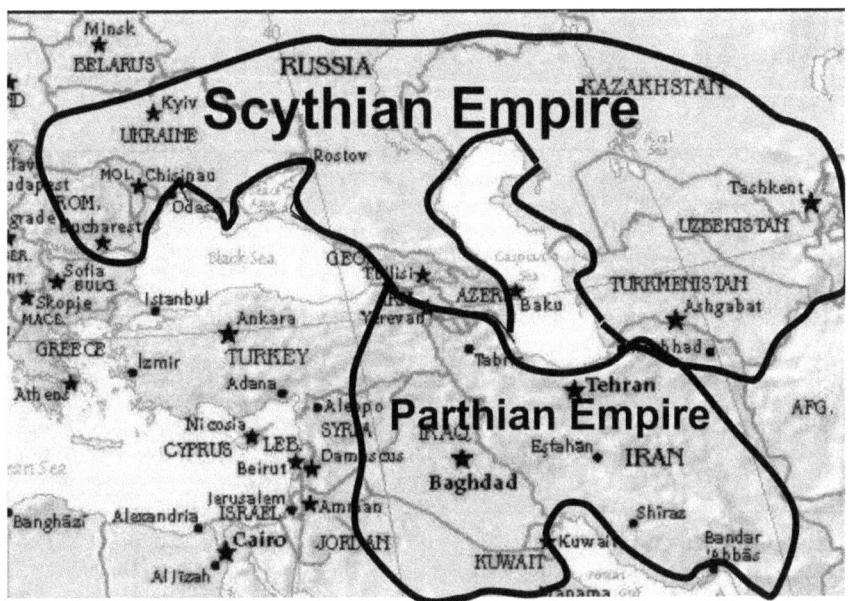

MAP 3: SCYTHIAN AND PARTHIAN TERRITORIES CIRCA 100 BC

Notes: Names of modern nations are included for reference. Basic map background courtesy of Free US CIA Factbook © 2008 maps by Michael Meuser at Mapcruzin.com

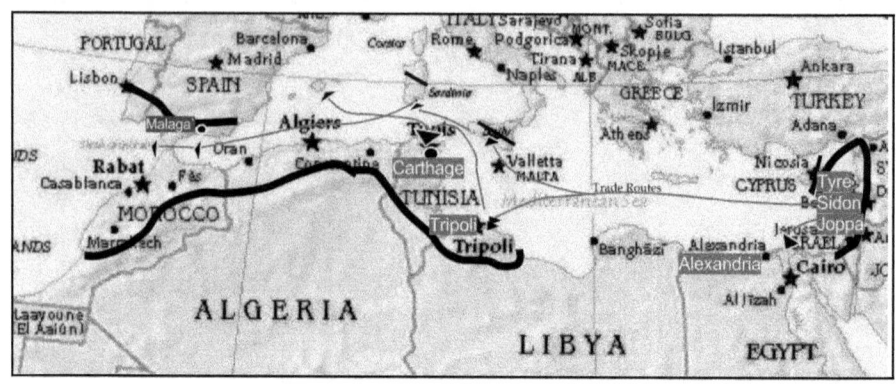

Map 4: Ancient Phoenician Empire

Notes: The Phoenician Empire was a group of related and working-together for positive trade and technological outcomes between 1200-700 BC. It included cities and ports from the black lines to the Mediterranean coast. Trade routes are marked. Major Phoenician cities are highlighted in Arial white lettering. Black lettering indicates modern day cities. Map courtesy of Free US CIA Factbook © 2008 maps by Michael Meuser at Mapcruzin.com Information verified on a great map with many more ancient cities marked that can be accessed at http://www.britannica.com/EBchecked/topic/457123/Phoenicia

4

IDENTIFYING 10-ISRAEL PART B

10-ISRAEL WHO ESCAPED INTO CARTHAGE.
In the same way that Phoenicians didn't call themselves by that name, the people of Carthage did not call themselves Carthaginians. Their enemy, Rome, gave them that name in their books. Since our history comes from Greco-Roman sources, "Carthage" is what we've been taught to call it, however, the name of this city upon its founding was "Kirjath-Hadeshath," which are Hebrew words meaning "new city."[1]

WHO WERE THESE ANCIENT CARTHAGINIANS/ NEW CITY-IANS? "The Carthaginians, like their Phoenician forebears, were excellent maritime navigators, traders and explorers."[1] Carthage was and is still located on the northern coast of Africa, just southeast of the "football" Italy's "boot" is kicking. (Isn't geography fun!) They were ruled by the "heads of state (who) were called Suffets...attested in Punic inscriptions as meaning 'judges' and obviously related to the Biblical Hebrew ruler title Shophet 'Judge')."[13(para 4)] The suffet judges held limited power though, since democratic (voting) elements were part of Carthage's rule, as well as a constitution. Interestingly, this mingled form of government is compared to that of Sparta and Crete.[13] (We established that Sparta was probably the "missing" Simeonites in chapter 3.)

Carthage was engaged with Rome in the Punic Wars. All the old Phoenician colonies of the coast of northern Africa and Iberia, including most of the Mediterranean Islands were now controlled by Carthage.

This sea-faring Carthaginian Empire doesn't seem to have stopped their ships at the Rock of Gibraltar at the mouth of the Mediterranean Sea though. Carthaginian coins have been found in America! Not only that, which I suppose could be an elaborate hoax, those coins have an etching of a "small set of easily-missed, minute markings at the bottom...When they are enlarged, a remarkable pattern emerges. (It is) a rudimentary map of the world known to the Carthaginians."[1(para 2)] It shows the Mediterranean Sea coast, including Spain, Europe, North Africa, with "two clumpings of islands to show where Corsica and Sardinia are located in the west and where Cyprus and Crete are located in the east. The British Isles are evident at the top of the map."[1(para 2)] Then to the west is a clump with three prongs. It doesn't look like America until you take into account the Carthaginians were "were excellent maritime navigators, traders and explorers. Their ships would have entered the 'navigable rivers' that even an ancient Greek writer (an enemy of Carthage) noted were present in North America."[1(para 3)] How would they have known the shape of those rivers unless they had sailed them? (A pretty amazing detailed picture can be studied here: http://phoenicia.org/america.html.)

These Carthaginian coins have been found as far away from Carthage as Britain, Spain, and the Americas (Albuquerque, New Mexico; Nevada, Ohio, Alabama and Georgia.[1]

Carthage had a fairly famous conqueror who nearly overcame Rome, Hannibal.[21] Hannibal's name was a combination of the Hebrew name Hananiah and the name Ba'al.[21] Remember Ba'al was mentioned in the Bible as a false god that 10-Israel struggled with time and time again before their exile. This name Hannibal sums up well what was going on at this time in 10-Israel's history: They were trying to combine their worship of the One True God and a false idol. They combined a Hebrew heritage with their idol Ba'al and tried to strike out on their own (though banded together) against the nation God had set in place to rule at that time (Rome). Obviously, God's plan and prophecies stood firm.

The point of studying Carthage and its wide-spread influence is to bring awareness of an empire founded and named in Hebrew that had a presence in the Americas 900-1000 years before Columbus (who was really a Moreno Jew named Christopher of Cologne, see chapter 10 of *Israel II: Beyond the Basics* for the full story) rediscovered the New World for Europe…who had apparently forgotten about it.

Won't heaven be fun when God tells us His true story of the world? I think we will be shaking our heads as we compare what we've been taught.

תא

The Ancient Parthians

The Parthi-who?

Modernly, the Parthians are little recognized, but they were an important somewhat-nomadic empire that flourished for 450 years from when they replaced the Persian and Seleucid Empires in 250 BC until 226 AD when they were conquered by the Sasonians.[12] Those dates place Jesus' earthly lifetime right in the center of their existence. The location of the Parthian Empire in modern-day Iran[12] makes them neighbors of the Seleucid-then-Macabee-then-Roman controlled Holy Land. But don't think of it just in context of modern-day Iran's current size. This Parthian Empire, in spite of its short 450 year existence, was very large in size stretching from the "Caucasus Mountains and Russian Steppes in the north (formerly the Scythian Empire) to the Persian Gulf and Indian Ocean in the south, and from the Euphrates River in the west to the Indus River in the east. Rome tried many times to conquer Parthia,"[17] but was never able to take over. So they don't bother to mention them much in their historical record.

> "Many are familiar with the account of the Magi worshipping the baby Jesus soon after his birth, but few are aware that the Magi were a delegation of Parthian nobles and the hereditary (Levite) priests of Parthia."
>
> –Steven Collins[18]

A group of related tribes in Parthia called "exiles in their Asian lands"[14] joined together and beat back the Seleucid Empire. Who do we know were exiled in Asia at this time that would also identify themselves as a "group of related tribes"? It was 10-Israel, still cooperating and living as one. Rawlinson records that the "Parthians were under the domination of the Assyrians and Medes prior to their becoming independent."[15] Interestingly, the cities of Parthia were called by Semitic names reflecting the clans of 10-Israel.[14] Some of those names include Samariane, obviously named for the conquered ancient capital Israelite city of Samaria; Gaza, the ancient Philistine city on Israel's coast; Asaak named for the second patriarch of Israel, Isaac; and Dara, perhaps named for the grandson of Judah mentioned in I Chronicles 2:6.[18]

The Parthian "Semitic kings often bore the name of the root-word "Phares," which identified the royal line of King David, who descended from Phares (I Chronicles 2:3-15)."[17 (para 6)] At least five of their kings used this name exclusively, Phares I-V.[19] These names of Parthian kings are part of fulfilled prophecy that David's descendants will rule over 10-Israel from Jeremiah 33:17.

Even the name "Iran" which is located in former Parthian territory, comes from the name of a 10-Israel clan, the "Eranites," from the 10-Israel Tribe of Ephraim (Numbers 26:35).[18] Teheran's (modern Iranian capital city) name is derived from this same clan.[18] "Of course, the modern Iranians are not Israelites. Iranians are descended from the Persians who later drove the Parthians out of Asia."[18(para 5)] But I think if Iran knew the connection to the names of their capitol's and nation's names, somebody in charge over there would be filing for a name change pretty quickly!

IDENTIFYING 10-ISRAEL PART B

חא

CIMMERIANS, CELTS, AND GAULS

The Anglo-Saxon population comes from the Cimmerians, the Celts and the Gauls in three distinct waves of western migration. Untwisting our history books can be done fairly easily by just using phonetics and knowing the development of a few key words.

CIMMERIANS is the easiest one of all. In our Bible "Cimmerians" is spelled "Samarians." Go ahead, sound it out. It is the same word! Cimmerians are the group of people descended from those who once lived in the capital city of Samaria, 10-Israel. However, after Judah finished her 70 year exile and returned home, she came across a few of the people who had survived behind 10-Israel's exile (200 years earlier by this time) and had intermarried with conquered people that Assyria had resettled in 10-Israel's land. Judah called these people Samaritans and refused to worship with them, and made them outcasts of society for at least 500 years up to Jesus' day (remember the Samaritan woman at the well?). Calling two separate groups of people by nearly the same name makes it awkward to try to explain where they went.

Originally the Cimmerians were known as *Khumri* to the Assyrians. They were renamed Gamira/Gamera and then Cimmerians.[24] The funny thing about the 'H' (as in kHumri) in many languages is that it can be hard, soft or absent in it pronunciation. And 'K' can be hard or absent too. The reason the Assyrians referred to the people they were conquering (10-Israel) as Khumri was related to a past king of 10-Israel who had made a name for himself about 100 years earlier. However our English translation Bible spells his name Omri (reigned in 10-Israel 876-879 BC). Language crossovers and spelling changes contribute greatly to the confusion surrounding the waves of exiles and people who just emigrated. During Omri's 12-year reign he accomplished several important things that set him up to be a memorable character in the minds of the Assyrians who would later refer to 10-Israel as "the House of Omri." (Omri moved the capital to Samaria and subdued the Moabites.)[27] For more than 200 years the Assyrians referred to the former Israelites as the "Khumeri" (i.e. the sons of Omri) or the "Bit Humri."

Later the Khumeri or "Kumri were known by the Greek(s) as the 'Kimbri,'" (who) are said to be the progenitors of the CELTS!"[24(para 19)] And since we get our history from Greco-Roman sources, what do you suppose we call them, but Celts. According to Samuel Lysons, "The Cimmerians seem...to be the same people [as] the Gauls or Celts under a different name; and it is observable that the Welsh, who are descended from the Gauls, still call themselves Cymri or Kymry" (*Our British Ancestors*, 1865, pp. 23, 27)."[24]

THE CELTS were the second wave of people from the east to begin migrating westward over land. Remember, the Phoenicians and others, such as some Greek colonies,[23] had already settled these modernly-called European areas, at least the coastal areas, arriving by sea back in and before Solomon's day. So there was a melding of cultures or a warring of cultures. The Celts did not record their history in written form. So, as we know from other experiences, whoever does the writing gets to tell the story. Contemporary Greeks wrote about the Celts, as did the Romans; they called them "barbarians." But the name-calling could have been borne of the wars they fought against one another. The Celts sacked "Rome at the end of the fourth century and (gained) a footing in Greece and Asia Minor in the third century. The Greeks called them 'Keltoi' and the Romans 'Galli'."[28(para2)]

THE GAULS[24] were a particular segment or tribe of the Cimmerian people. The Gauls' name for themselves was *Kymris*, "but the Romans labeled them *Celts, Galli, Gallus* and *Galates* (Galatians). The

Hellenistic and Roman conquerors (300 BC-AD 200) renamed the area of Gilead, once home of the exiled Israelite tribes of Gad, Reuben and half of Manasseh, *Gaulanitis.* "[24(para 27)] Why all this Gaul-related naming? If we look at the meaning of the word *gaul*, it brings a deeper level of understanding.

The word *gaul* comes from the Hebrew word *galah* which means "carried captive." Interestingly, whether the word is in Latin (*gallo* or *gallus*) or Celtic (*galler* or *waller*) or German (*waller* or *walah*) or even in French (*gaullois*) it carries the same meaning as the original Hebrew, "stranger, traveler or exile."[24] Both *Golan* (of Golan Heights, Israel) and *Galatia* (of Paul's letter to the Galatians) are related to living outside of Israel's borders in exile. The "exile" is evident from their name. Remember Hosea's prophecy that 10-Israel would be wanderers (Hosea 9:17)? Not only does 10-Israel conform to this word, wandering westward century after century, but they are even called for a time by this name: the Gauls (the wanderers)!

> Ancient writers spoke of the Gauls, who gave their name to modern-day France, as the "Cimbri," and identified them with the Cimmerians of an earlier date, who are mentioned by Homer. They are identified as migrating through the mouth of the Danube, and early Celts are said to have been "continually moving westward." The "Belgae" were also Cimbri in origin. They spread across the Rhine and gave their name "to all northern France and Belgium" (*Encyclopedia Britannica*, 11th edition, Vol. 5, page 612).[as quoted by 24]

So, all three of these groups the Cimmerians, the Celts and the Gauls, were settling Europe out of their Middle Eastern origins from the time of the 10-Israel exile and forward. Let's take a look at who these civilizations became and see if we can find individual tribes of Israel among them.

MAP 5: THE MOVEMENTS OF 10-ISRAEL BEGINNING AT THE ASSYRIAN INVASION OF 722 BC.

Note: Names of modern nations are included in black for reference. The white lettering denotes the tribes and empires who either *were* Israel in exile (Scythia, Massagetea, Samarians, & Parthia) or who hosted them in their empires (Bactria, Media, Assyria and later Babylonia in place of Assyria & Media).

PART 2

IDEAS ON WHERE SPECIFIC TRIBES CAN BE FOUND TODAY

Though much of the world, including a majority of Christians have believed that the 10 tribes of Israel's northern kingdom have been lost to history's migrations and intermarriage, it is important to know that when God says something, He means it. His Word is a promise to mankind, and we can trust everything He says. When he said that 12,000 from each tribe of Israel would be sealed in Zion, He knew the tribes would be scattered and He would draw them back to Him. He never "lost" them, and is not worried that they are still all over the globe and most do not know who they are any more.

Levi and Judah are fairly easy for us to trace because they held onto their identity by following the Law of God. "There seems to be a general consensus that the British are Ephraim, the USA is Manasseh, the French are Reuben, the Dutch are Zebulon, the Jews/Israelis are Judah, etc."[20(para4)] But by tracing tribal migrations and using clues that God inserted into His Word in Genesis 49 and Deuteronomy 33 through the prophetic blessing of the sons of Jacob which specifically describes them in the last days, we can follow God's bread crumbs in almost treasure map accuracy to find the "Lost Tribes" of Israel!

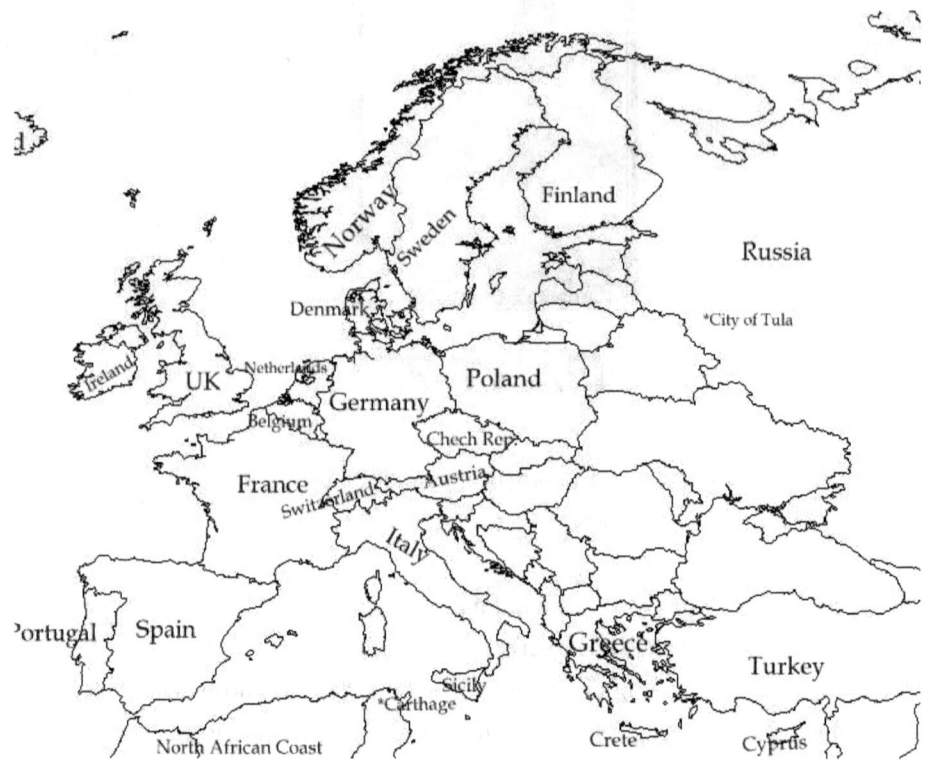

Map 6: Modern Europe

Notes: For reference in the following chapters that describe where the tribes of 10-Israel are hidden today.

5

GAD AND REUBEN

GAD FOUND IN (FORMER) WEST GERMANY[20]

Gad was the seventh son of Jacob, his first with Leah's maid Zilpah. Gad and Asher were full brothers. His name means "troop." In the Promised Land Gad received an inheritance on the east side of the Jordan River, south of ½ Manasseh.

PROPHETIC DESCRIPTIONS

Genesis 49 and Deuteronomy 33 are both prophetic descriptions of the tribe of Gad we can use to find them in these latter days.

> **Genesis 49:19** (NKJV) Gad, a troop shall tramp upon him, But he shall triumph at last.

> **Genesis 49:19** (GW) Gad will be attacked by a band of raiders, but he will strike back at their heels.

> **Deuteronomy 33:20-21** And of Gad he said: "Blessed *is* he who enlarges Gad; He dwells as a lion, And tears the arm and the crown of his head. [21] He

provided the first *part* for himself, Because a lawgiver's portion was reserved there. He came *with* the heads of the people; He administered the justice of the LORD, And His judgments with Israel."

ASSYRIAN INVASION

The tribe of Gad was among the tribes taken captive to Assyria in the first wave. It is likely that they (with Reuben and ½ Manasseh) were resettled in the eastern-most area of the Assyrian Empire to discourage reunification with 10-Israel's might.[20]

When searching for modern-day Gad, according to the above prophecies, we are looking for a large, well-assimilated nation. Gad will be a nation that "dwells as a lion, tearing the arm and crown of the head" or in today's terms Gad will be predatory and very militaristic.[20] His name even means troop. Gad will be one who has had a troop trample him, but he has triumphed at the last days. The God's Word translation uses "band of raiders" instead of "troop," making it sound as though some sort of alliance was/will be formed to overcome Gad. Gad will be an administrator of the Lord's justice (not man's view of justice) of Israel.

There is just one nation that fulfills all these descriptions: Germany. (Think World War II: the aggressor who was brought down by the Allies). And more specifically, West Germany. Here is how we can get that specific: Gad (+ Reuben and ½ Manasseh) assimilated into Assyria, and Genesis 10:21-22 says that Assyria was a Semitic nation too, meaning that physical and racial differences would have been minute. Assyria, after its defeat and dozens of centuries, migrated slowly west becoming the Prussians of Europe. Reuben became France.[20] A trio of wars set up the Prussian territories to be the leading province in the German Empire.[22] The Prussian Kingdom, after WWII, was abolished (1947) absorbing the people and territory into what we now call Germany[22]...East Germany. Since Prussia (former Assyrians) is found in East Germany, it brings us to an even more specific location of 10-Israel's Gad in West Germany.

½ MANASSEH AMONG GAD. Many of ½ Manasseh from Assyria became part of Germany, while the ½ Manasseh who left 10-Israel later ended up in Britain. But for prophecy to be fulfilled Manasseh must be reunified as one tribe from this split that occurred so long ago. Think back to a story that did make most of our history books to just before the Revolutionary War in the United States. Settlers had been drawn to America from two primary places en masse: Britain and Germany. In fact there is an old wives' tale that it was so evenly halved that when the American Congress voted for a common language in which to conduct government and be our "official language," a single vote decided that The Declaration of Independence would be written in English, not German. While that did *not* actually happen, that the story was circulated and believed, itself points to a large contingent of German speaking people and leaders in America.

Both Steven Collins and Yair Davidy, author of *Israelite Origins of Western People*, contend that much of Manasseh lived in Germany for a time, but for the most part "it largely migrated to the early USA...Even as Manasseh was split in two halves which were physically separated from each other for millennia, these halves" [20(para9)] have been reunited in the United States.

When ½ Manasseh left east and west Germany, the tribe of Gad remained (unbeknownst to them, but very known to God and according to His plan set up before the foundation of the earth.). Back in the Genesis 48-49-era God poured out the Birthright Blessing on Joseph's sons, Manasseh and Ephraim, but the rest of Israel still received a blessing as sons of Abraham.

> At the end of World War II, Germany was occupied and split into Western and Eastern Germany. West Germany "overcame" its defeat and became a very prosperous ally of Ephraim and Manasseh and many other Israelite tribes in NATO. West Germany shared in the Abrahamic

blessings poured out on the Western World after World War II along with many other Israelite tribes, but the Eastern Germans (cut off on the eastern side of the Soviet Iron Curtain) did not receive them. This indicates that God knew exactly which portion of Germany was dominated by an Israelite tribe (Gad), and which part was dominated by non-Israelites (the Assyrians).[20(para 11)]

Since these prophecies of Genesis and Deuteronomy were specifically given to identify and locate 10-Israel in the last days, we can determine with specificity that the tribe of Gad can be found in West Germany.

חא

REUBEN IS FOUND IN FRANCE

Reuben was the firstborn son of Jacob and Leah. His name means "see a son" (Genesis 29:32). Reuben begins his life being a demand for Leah's personal honor because she was loved less than Rachel.[23] Throughout his lifetime Reuben tried to execute his role as firstborn, failing so many times. First, though he saved Joseph from the other brothers' plot to kill him, Reuben failed to return and pull Joseph out of the cistern before the brothers sold him. He was too late. Second, he slept with his father's concubine dishonoring Jacob/Israel and lost his birthright as oldest son. Third, Reuben offered a solution in the matter with bringing Benjamin to Egypt to get food for the family and his solution was immediately rejected (Genesis 42:36-38). Usually Reuben's failure came because he was slow to act.

Reuben was a natural firstborn, offering solutions, moving on what he believes is due him in his place of honor, trying to lead the others, but he never quite succeeded as a true firstborn should. Reuben's being slow to act became a character trait that was passed on to his descendants; so also did his propensity for sexual sin get passed on.

Prophetic Blessing and Description of Reuben in Last Days

Even though Reuben dishonored his father and lost out on his birthright, he was not dismissed from the blessing of being a son of Abraham, Isaac and Israel. Here is the prophetic word spoken over Reuben and his descendants.

> **Genesis 49:3-4** "Reuben, you are my firstborn, My might and the beginning of my strength, The excellency of dignity and the excellency of power. 4 Unstable as water, you shall not excel, Because you went up to your father's bed; Then you defiled *it*— He went up to my couch.

Another interesting but strange—almost a prophetic prayer—blessing is bestowed on Reuben when Moses is blessing the tribes before he dies.

> **Deuteronomy 33:6** Let Reuben live, and not die, *Nor* let his men be few.

The tribe of Reuben after settling in the Promised Land exhibited some characteristics that point toward a future fullness that is less than desirable. They separated themselves on the far side of the Jordan River, choosing to receive their inheritance there. When the Judge Deborah called the men of Israel to war, Reuben was slow to act. In her Victory Song, Deborah says of Reuben,

> **Judges 5:15b-16** Among the divisions of Reuben *There were* great resolves of heart. 16 Why did you sit among the sheepfolds, To hear the pipings for the flocks? The divisions of Reuben have great searchings of heart.

Deborah judged the men of Reuben to be sitting around thinking great, beautiful, pastoral thoughts, playing music for their sheep and searching their hearts (for great thoughts of passion perhaps), and ones who would not involve themselves in the defense of Israel.

French Character and History

We know the French descended from the branch of the Celts called the Gauls,[25] that is in our current history books. Earlier we established where those Celts and Gauls are related back to tribes of 10-Israel as they migrated across Europe. Let's look at Reuben's sons and their Hebrew name meanings[24] while thinking of French people being descended from the tribe of Reuben: From Genesis 46:9, the sons of Reuben are Hanoch, Pallu, Hezron, and Carmi.

Hanoch means "dedicated."
Pallu means "separated and distinguished."
Hezron means "enclosed" or "surrounded by a wall."
Carmi means "vinedresser."

"All of the above names acquire an additional significance when considered in the light of French history and culture."[24] The names of Reuben's sub-tribes are descriptive as a whole of the modern nation of France and the empires they descended from. (See source 26 for more details).

Demand for personal pride, vanity, finery. When we think of the best of the best in food, culture, wine, ballet, fashion, who do we think of? France. Even a French phrase is used to describe the best, the *crème de la crème*. The French are distinguished in things of finery. They indulge themselves (to the point of snobbishness). And when others want to indulge themselves, they go to France. The French

> have the characteristics of being passionate, sensitive, unstable, cultured, refined, seekers of justice, daring, etc.

The French believe in ceremonial. They also hold to rigidity of rights, e.g. people who pass certain examinations, who are born into certain families, etc, have automatic rights to positions of governmental service and the like. There is less allowance for a free flow of enterprise and talent. They have the characteristics of a dispossessed first-born son of basically good nature but who can never quite reconcile himself with what he has lost.[23(para 13)]

SEXUAL SIN. The French are world renown for being lovers, and usually marriage is not involved. This propensity toward sexual sin is a generational sin and a character weakness passed down from their forefather, Reuben.

INSTABILITY. France's government has been flipping right then left and back again for hundreds of years now. In the French Revolution (1788-1799), people, especially leaders, were losing their heads left and right. With as many who died in this tumultuous time in France's history, it is the blessing Moses prayed a couple of millennia earlier that "Reuben would not die out" which kept a remnant alive, preserved.

TRIES TO TAKE LEAD BUT IS DENIED by true birthright owners Manasseh and Ephraim. During the exploration of the "new world" France led the way at one time. Perhaps reaping the benefit of Jacob's blessing "my might and the <u>beginning</u> of my strength" but quickly lost influence and favor in the U.S. to the Germans and British (Ephraim and Manasseh) the true birthright holders.

REFUSAL TO ACT. In WWII France got steam-rolled by the Nazis because they refused to stand up to them. Whether it was national pride that made the French think the Nazis wouldn't dare take over or whether it was self-imposed blindness that kept them from doing something, the fact remains, France and their government and noblemen waited too long to act in their own defense or the defense of Europe, just like the tribe of Reuben refused to act in defense of Israel under Deborah.

The sons of Reuben in France as they follow their prophetic description will have dignity, and power, but because they are as "unstable as water," they will never maintain a leadership position in the world.[26] "We can see in these aspects of the French character the qualities of a first-born son who is conscious of the innate rights he should receive and feels that the rest of the world should be governed along the same principles."[23] These characteristics are from the eldest son Reuben who lost his birthright due to sin and have been passed down generation to generation in France.

6

DAN AND BENJAMIN

TRIBE OF DAN BECOMES THE IRISH AND DANES

Dan was born to Jacob and Bilhah (Rachel's servant), and the simple meaning of his name is "judge." However there is more to it than that (as usual with Hebrew words). The Pulpit Commentary says because of the meaning of Dan's name he "should occupy an important place and exercise highly beneficial functions in the future commonwealth, enjoying independence and self-government as one of the tribes of Israel...and performing the office of an administrator among the People not of his own tribe merely, but also of all Israel"[31(as quoted by Salemi)] So more than just "judge," Dan is related to governing and government of Israel.

The prophetic word in Genesis 49 over Dan, the fifth son of Jacob/Israel given at Jacob's death.

> **Genesis 49:16-18** "Dan shall judge his people As one of the tribes of Israel. ¹⁷ Dan shall be a serpent by the way,

> A viper by the path, That bites the horse's heels So that its rider shall fall backward. ¹⁸ I have waited for your salvation, O LORD!

There are some interesting aspects of Dan listed in this Latter Days prophecy. The anointing of judgment that Dan carries is easily evident and requires no interpretation. But the middle part about serpents and vipers and biting horse heels, is a little trickier. "The meaning of this prophecy is that he would leave a trail wherever he would go. The evidence of this is clear. Dan's migrations as revealed in the Bible, shows them naming everything after their father 'Dan,'"[31(para3)] from Joshua 19:47 and Judges 18. I admit I had a little trouble making the leap of interpretation from serpents, vipers, biting a horse, and a rider falling backward with the tribe using the name Dan until I read Yair Davidiy's explanation which refers "to a Tribal Trait of leaving their namesake everywhere like the trail of a snake print showing the wriggling of his passage"[32(para titled "4")] as the tribe of Dan did as they made their way westward over the centuries.

The final Genesis 49 prophetic word has Dan declaring that he has waited for God's salvation. This can only take place if Dan has not experienced God's salvation. But eventually Dan will, based on God's promises:

> **Jeremiah 31:1**: "At the same time," says the Lord, "I will be the God of <u>all the families of Israel</u>, and they shall be My people."
>
> **Romans 11:26** And so <u>all Israel will be saved</u>, as it is written: "The Deliverer will come out of Zion, And He will turn away ungodliness from Jacob;

DEBORAH'S SONG about the tribes of Israel during the period of the judges asks the question "Why did Dan remain on ships?" (Judges 5:17b), instead of coming to aid their brothers in defeating the enemy who was attacking Israel at this time. This was a pivotal time in Israel's existence as they were being established in the Promised Land, yet Dan had isolated themselves, pursuing their own agenda, like many of the other tribes who were also lashed by Deborah's song.

Growing up in the western Christian church, my first thought years ago in reading this was, What was Dan doing on ships in the first place? Israel is a desert! But of course when a map is consulted, anyone can see where Dan received their inheritance, it is obvious: Dan got beach front property. Of course they would be out sailing on ships.

LOCATION OF TRIBAL INHERITANCE

Joshua 19:40-48 describes Dan's inheritance in a list of towns located in the southwest of the Promised Land, including the coastal city of Joppa. Joppa has sprawled north into the current large coastal city of Tel Aviv. Dan shows their fortitude and pioneer spirit right away by going after more towns which were outside of their original territory:

> **Joshua 19:47** And the border of the children of Dan went beyond these, because the children of Dan went up to fight against Leshem and took it; and they struck it with the edge of the sword, took possession of it, and dwelt in it. They called Leshem, Dan, after the name of Dan their father.

Interesting that barely settled into their territory, the tribe of Dan is already leaving their mark, their name, on their new place. Then, being next to the Mediterranean Sea, Dan took to the great waters. Their new city of Dan (formerly Lashem) was only 30 miles from Tyre a huge seafaring city-state of the Phoenicians, occupied by Dan's brothers, the tribe of Asher. "In 2 Chronicles 2:14 we see Danites dwelling (in) the city of Tyre. These people of Tyre were a people of sea trade and navigation."[31(para 7)] We saw in Deborah's Song that the Dan-ites were so concentrated on their sea trade they wouldn't help their brothers, but where were they sailing? Well, Greece for one. Three different sources go into great detail to prove that the Hellenes of Greece and the Israelite

Semites were closely related! (see note 33). Ezekiel 27 easily places Dan in trade with Greece. (Javan is the Biblical name for Greece.)

> **Ezekiel 27:12-13a** "Tarshish *was* your merchant because of your many luxury goods. They gave you silver, iron, tin, and lead for your goods. [13] Javan, Tubal, and Meshech *were* your traders.

While the rest of the Ezekiel 27 above is not flattering at all for Tyre, this lengthy lament does offer historical evidence that Tyre, occupied by Asher and Dan, was in trade with Greece and other cities along the Mediterranean coast, and therefore they were quite mobile in their ships.

Westward in three waves Dan becomes part of the Greeks, the Irish, and the Danes

The first wave of Dan-ites appears to have left the company of Israel as the Egypt Exodus was taking place.[33] Joining themselves with the people of Greece (some of the people Dan would later trade with.), those who went maintained their separate history, and slightly later perhaps hosted the Spartans (Simeonites) in their lands.[35] This Dan-ite tribe, at that time called *Danaan*, lived along side and with the Greeks for two centuries while trading with Israel proper (and other cultures) including the tribe of Dan which had remained with Moses, and they all had ships, intermingling.

Then a group of Dan-at-Greece (*Danaan*) migrated further westward in those ships. One wave of explorers sailed to Ireland establishing colonies there. They were called *"Tuatha de Danaan."*[35] Greco-Roman history refers to the entire colonization of western Europe and (British) Islands as a Phoenician enterprise. But we have seen already that several waves of migration included various tribes of 10-Israel; 10-Israel mingled with other peoples from Mediterranean coastal lands forming what we call the Phoenician Empire. But remember they didn't call themselves that. There was not a single great emperor over all these "Phoenician" lands calling the shots. There were lots of smaller tribes with their own leadership and their own ideas and transportation to help them explore those ideas.

Another wave of land-based westward migration moved first northward to Scythia with portions of some of the other tribes before the time of the Assyrian invasion. Eventually the Dan-ites [called *Dingling* and *Dangalai* (meaning Dan of Galilee) at the time] moved on further and further west, across Europe, through present-day Germany until finding their final resting place in Denmark and becoming the Danes. Their trail across Europe is marked by their name, Dan, left on the geography. "The Irish are the descendants of the Danites who sailed to ancient Ireland (*Danaan*). Both the Irish and Danes have a strong maritime history, as one would expect of Danites (Judges 5:17)."[38(para 5)]

Collins offers a prophetic-fulfillment explanation of why Dan is not mentioned with the other tribes at the Assyrian invasions of the 700's BC. In Deuteronomy 33:22, Moses prophesies, "Dan *is* a lion's whelp; He shall leap from Bashan." Interestingly, the area known as Bashan is where the *inland* Danites dwelt.[37] It is probable, according to historical evidence, that the Dan-ites had already decided to "leap" out of Bashan toward the Black Sea region to avoid the Assyrians.[37]

A later group of Dan-ites migrated from 10-Israel around the time of Jeremiah, stopping in Greece (perhaps to visit relatives still there?) and then traveled on to Spain, before landing permanently in Ireland. This group of *Danaan* carried with them part of the Royal family of the line of David, and they set up a throne in the city of Tara.[35,30] (perhaps named after Terah, Abraham's father.) "It is certainly no coincidence that the Irish Gaelic word *Dun* or *Dunn* means "Judge," just as *Dan* does in Hebrew!"[35]

> Danes from Dan were recorded together with the Naphtali in Scythia. From Scythia the Danes (moving via Sweden) conquered Denmark. The Danes and the Norwegians formed the Vikings who invaded England.

> The Danes settled in the northeast of England and the Norwegians in the northwest. They also conquered and settled in Ireland and in parts of Scotland.[31]

The Dan-ites really got around! It is evident from the very beginning of their record that they were on the move, always pioneering ahead.

DAN LEAVES A TRAIL OF FOREFATHER DAN written everywhere they go. Beginning with their first conquered and renamed city Lashem to Dan, the Danites leave the name Dan (or DN without the vowel sound as it would have been written in ancient times) on everything. When Dan continued north and became associated with the name Scythians, the "rivers emptying into the Black Sea region used to be named Ister, Tyras, the Borysthenes and Tanais. After they arrived there, the names of the rivers were changed to Danube, the Dnestr, (Danaper) and the Don" [34] p.434 as they remain to this day.

Names such as Damnae, also called "Dingling" were linked to the "Dangalai" whose name means "Dan of Galilee." Damnonii of Scotland (who lived beside the northern River Don of Scotland) and the Damnones of Dannonia (Devon and Cornwall) are other names where Dan shows up. The tribe of Dana ("Tuatha de Danaan") in Ireland, Damnonii in Scotland, the city of Danum, and Denmark and the Danes are all related to the Dan-ites' trail.[31] When viewing all these ancient and current Dens, Dans, and Dons together it is easy to see the lasting impression the tribe of Dan has made in cities and geography of the world.

> Denmark, the name of the modern country in Europe north of Germany, means, literally, "Dan's mark." Its people are called "Danes." In fact, because at one time Denmark ruled all the surrounding region, the whole region took its name from them, the ScanDINavian peninsula! Clearly, here are remnants of the people of DAN, who migrated westward overland from the Caucasus to their present location in northern Europe!

"According to late Danish tradition... Jutland [the mainland of Denmark] was acquired by DAN, the... ancestor of the DANES" from whom their name derives ("Denmark," *Encyclopaedia Britannica,* 11th ed., vol.8). The Danes claim the(y) descend from "Dan the Great" meaning Dan of Israel (Saxo Grammaticus; The First Nine Books of Saxo Grammaticus of the Danish History).[31]

Even the shape of the latter day country of Denmark is shaped like a serpent's head! How exact is that Genesis 49 word now?

NEED MORE OF DAN'S SNAKE PATH? Consider names such as Dans-Lough, Dan-Sower, Dan-Monism, Dun-dalke, Dun-drum, Don-egal Bay, Don-egal City, Dun-glow, Lon-don-derry, Din-gle, Dun-garven and Duns-more, which incidentally means "more Dans."[35]

A JUDGE OVER HIS BROTHERS, YET HIS OWN NATION. Where is the Hague, the UN tribunal court? International Court of Justice and International Criminal Court? In Dutch it is called "Den Haag." Can you see Dan written on its name? Den Haag is currently located in the Netherlands, but was once part of Denmark, as was all of *Scan*dinavia. In the name *Scandinavia* we can see the S-K sound of Isaac and Scythia paired with the "din" of the tribe of Dan. The tribe of Dan has left its mark in Scandinavia as well and with so many international courts (judges) residing in Den Haag, there is a remaining connection with Dan who is the judge of Israel.

IRISH/POLICE CONNECTION [31]
Another way the "judge" and "administrating" or "governing" of Dan's name comes into play while the 19th-21st centuries unfold shows up when the Irish began to migrate even further west to the United States. Irish immigrants quickly found employment in fields of civil service becoming firefighters and policemen in the Northeast and Great Lakes areas. In New York, "by the turn of the 20th century, five out of six NYPD officers were Irish born or of Irish descent. As late as the 1960s,

even after minority hiring efforts, 42% of the NYPD were Irish Americans."[31 para 2 "Prophecy Fulfilled"] This is Dan fulfilling his God-given destiny from a prophetic word 3000 years ago!

SAMPSON AND HERCULES CONNECTION

Just a short teaser to introduce a real-life hero for you superhero lovers out there. Have you ever noticed the similarities between the Biblical record of the judge Sampson who happens to be from the tribe of Dan and the story/legend of Hercules? Even *Encyclopedia of the Classical World* mentions that Hercules is based on the exploits of an historic figure.[35] A couple similarities to get you started: Both Hercules and Sampson were super-human strong, almost invincible, both killed a lion with their bare hands, both figures have trouble escaping the clutches of a woman.[35] But Sampson and Hercules don't even sound similar! So where did the name difference come from?

> The word Hercules in Greek is, "Heracles," which is virtually identical with the Hebrew plural word for *traders*, "Heraclim," and Heracles is said to have come from "Argos," himself! The Greek myths tell that the people of Argos are from the Danioi were descended from a patriarch "Danaos" who was the son of "Bela." In the Bible, the Hebrew patriarch Dan was the son of the concubine "Bilhah" (Genesis 30:3-6).[35(para 4 "The Mighty Hercules")]

Check out http://www.british-israel.ca/Dan.htm or www.britam.org for more exciting details.

SUMMARY OF DAN IN THE LAST DAYS

The "lost" tribe of Dan went out in splinter groups and became both the Danes of Denmark and the Irish of Eire (Ireland) and some migrated to the United States.

חא

DAN AND BENJAMIN

BENJAMIN BECOMES NORMANS AND VIKINGS IN NORWAY AND ICELAND

Benjamin was the baby of the family. He was the 12th son of Jacob/Israel and the 2nd son of the beloved wife Rachel, who died giving birth to him. His name means "son of my right hand" (Genesis 35:18) with "right hand" denoting a place of power.[42] Whomever sits at the right hand of a ruler has power to influence the king and power in his own right within the realm to bring about the ruler's desires. With the sons of Joseph (Ephraim and Manasseh) receiving the birthright, birthrate and power from Jacob/Israel's blessing, it seems right that Joseph's only full blood brother would receive the blessing of being seated at the right hand of that birthright of ruling the earth.[42]

One of the first stories of Benjamin is when he was protected by his father Israel and not allowed to go to Egypt with his brothers. It taught his brothers to be careful with him, to protect him. This care continues on even through the latter days. Moses' prophecy about Benjamin shows this too. "Benjamin became the protected son of Israel, and in prophecy we see this protection continuing into the end time," [42]

> **Deuteronomy 33:12** And of Benjamin he said, The beloved of the LORD shall dwell in safety by him; and the LORD shall cover him all the day long, and he shall dwell between his shoulders".[42]

The Genesis 49 blessing or prophecy of character Jacob/Israel gives over Benjamin on his deathbed is this:

> **Genesis 49:27** Benjamin is a ravenous wolf; In the morning he shall devour the prey, And at night he shall divide the spoil.

That word sure makes Benjamin sound like a fierce fighter. It goes well with a story about the time of the judges in Israel when Benjamin was foolish enough to fight all the other tribes of Israel at once (Judges 19-21). Surprisingly the first two of three battles were huge wins for Benjamin. Outnumbered 400,000 to 26,700, the Benjamites killed 40,000 Israelites. When Israel turned to God with fasting and prayer though, in the end, Benjamin was decimated with only 600 men remaining! From that time forward their population numbers were far behind the other tribes.

Interestingly, when Benjamin had to find wives, God arranged for wives to be found in the Ephraimite city of Shiloh. Shiloh was the only city absent when Israel's men vowed not to give their daughters in marriage to Benjamin. Ephraim was one (of only two) of Benjamin's closest genetic matches to rebuild their population, because Ephraim and Manasseh were Joseph's sons, and Joseph was a full blooded brother to Benjamin.

Later in an unexpected move, God had Samuel anoint a Benjamite, Saul, as the first king of Israel (I Samuel 9:21), before He moved to the tribe of Judah as the dynasty of leadership preserved for Israel. (Perhaps this was because God was really the King of Israel and one of the tribe of Benjamin was functioning as His "right hand" man.) When Israel was cleaved in two, it was Benjamin who stayed by Judah's side. Benjamin's inheritance was even located to the east of Judah, which is the "right hand" to Judah's kings when looking at a map.

When Judah went into captivity, Benjamin was still by her right hand (I Kings 12:21). Seventy years later when a remnant of Judah returned, Benjamin was also a part of that remnant, still by Judah's side, helping restore the walls of Jerusalem and the splendor of the Promised Land after the punishment was over (Ezra 1:5; Nehemiah 11:3-4). Also like Judah, 90% of Benjamin chose to remain in exile, living abroad in Babylon. The only tribes in exile that sent a remnant back to rebuild Judea were Judah, Benjamin and Levi. They eventually covered the land of Israel and Judah, Samaria and the Galilee, with Benjamin residing in the north (Nehemiah 11:31-35). "Herbert Hannay's book, *European and Other Race Origins,* included ancient records that "representatives of Benjaminites spread over the whole length and breadth of Asia Minor.'"[41(para 3)] These were the families that did not return from the exile.

An example of tribes still living abroad during the Apostolic period is Rabbi Sha'ul aka Saul of Tarsus. He was born in Tarsus which was located in Asia Minor. He did however make journeys to/from Jerusalem throughout his lifetime.

> Jesus was a Jew, of the tribe of Judah, (Rev 5:5; John 4:9). And the Bible says, "He came unto his own, and his own received him not." (John 1:11). The Jews of Judah rejected him, but the Galileans received him gladly, "But as many as received him [Galileans], to them gave he power to become the sons of God, *even* to them that believe on his name:" (v.12). During his boyhood years, and most of his 3 ½ (years of) ministry, he spent it in Galilee, in Benjamin's land.[42(para 39)]

Benjamin in Galilee was separated and cared for by God, who gave them revelation of who Yeshua was. Many of the 12 disciples came from Benjamin.

In 70 AD after many riots that had been quelled by Rome throughout their rule, the final battle began as Rome swept down from the north, Benjamite Galilee, eventually ending in the burning of Jerusalem. You might think that this sweeping of Benjamin completely did away with this tribe, but no! There was a prophetic word given by Jeremiah, years earlier.

> **Jeremiah 6:1** "O you children of Benjamin, Gather yourselves to flee from the midst of Jerusalem! Blow the trumpet in Tekoa, And set up a signal-fire in Beth Haccerem; For disaster appears out of the north, And great destruction.

The Benjamites, who had received the revelation of Yeshua took this warning seriously and fled the land of Israel before all were massacred. When they fled, they took the good news of Yeshua with them! Most went east to Pella[42] and a few escaped south to Judea to warn them. These Benjamites who fled to Pella were the first Messianic Jews. They eventually migrated to rejoin their brother Benjamites in Asia Minor (the 90% which had remained abroad) though a few went back into Israel.[42]

After a couple of centuries though, the Persians began to push the Parthians into Armenia crowding Benjamin's lands and Benjamin began migrating north into Dacia.[42] Dacia was located in the mountains north of Greece and west of the Black Sea, today known as the Balkan Region or Romania and Bulgaria.[42] Dacians are described as being tall, with very fair skin, straight, light hair and light eyes.[42] Their name comes from the word *Daoi*, the Phyrgian word for wolf.[42] Benjamin's sign was a wolf (like Judah's was a lion and Naphtali's was a gazelle),[43] and it corresponds with the word given in Genesis 49, "Benjamin, the ravenous wolf."

> The city of Daous-dava, in Lower Moesia, between the Danube and Mount Haemus, literally meant "village of wolves." Formerly, then, the Dacians called themselves "wolves" or "those who are like wolves," who resemble wolves... The very symbol of the Dacians was the "wolf."[42]

From their place in the Balkans, Benjamin kept moving west- and northward, though traces of them are scarce until they pop up a couple hundred years later in a way we can recognize from their symbols, character and relative size (to the other tribes now occupying Western Europe).

> Genesis 49's clues can include geographic clues, but most of them address various cultural and/or historical traits which can be linked to modern nations in the latter days. ... The clue for Norway does point to a northern

location by likening Benjamin to a wolf as wolves are typical of northern climates.[40(para 4)]

VIKINGS FROM NORWAY

The name Norman as applied to people from Norway means North-man.[42] The Normans or Norsemen were formerly the Dacians. "In the tenth century Dudo, who wrote the earliest history of the Normans, plainly says they were the Dacians from the Balkans."[42(para 5 titled "The Dacians")] The Norman, William the Conqueror used a wolf as his symbol.[45] The Normans were known as Sea-wolves.[25]

> The phrases about "devouring the prey" and "dividing the spoil" do not describe today's Norwegians, but they very aptly describe Norway's well-known Viking heritage. The Vikings were known for preying (in raiding parties akin to wolfpacks) on all the other nations of Europe from bases in their northern coastlands. This parallels ancient times. Even as Benjamin warred against all the other tribes of Israel in a bloody civil war in biblical times, the Vikings also raided and preyed upon all the other tribes of Israel who had migrated to various locations in Europe.[41(para 8)]

The Vikings preyed like wolves on most of Europe, and also made their way to the Americas. "It is well known that the Normans, who settled in northern France, were Vikings from Norway, and they were largely of the tribe of Benjamin, (though Dan from Denmark did join with them for their exploits and exploring) which may be inferred from their heraldry."[25(para 28-30)]. The Vikings moved to settle in Iceland[42] led by Rollo (or Rolf) and also went from Norway into Normandy and Scotland which is where they picked up the name "Normans"[42] by which we refer to them today.

In Scotland we can find the name Ross which was also the name of a tribe of Benjamin (Rosh) .[42] The 'sh' and 's' are interchangeable in

Hebrew since they are the same letter: sheen. In Normandy (part of France) we find the Namnetes "who derived their name from Naaman, a son of Benjamin."[42]

Some of the Normans who settled in France ended up migrating to Canada and populating Quebec.[42]

LEFT HANDED VIKINGS

According to *National Geographic* the Vikings "trained themselves in sword fighting using the left hand. Some have recorded that the Vikings fought well with the left hand as well as the right."[44 (p.11)] Does this sound familiar? The Benjamites are described the same way in Judges 3:15 and 20:15-16. Among Benjamin were 700 mighty fighting men who were left-handed.

"BETWEEN THE SHOULDERS"

When we revisit the Deuteronomy promise about Benjamin, he is called the "beloved of the Lord," it says Benjamin will "dwell in safety," the Lord will cover him and Benjamin "shall dwell between his shoulders" (Deuteronomy 33:12). We saw how in days past Benjamin heeded the word of the Lord from Jeremiah and escaped north to safety. But how does a tribe "dwell between the shoulders"? It could be a double meaning. Between shoulders can refer to the borders or edges of a land.[42] The Pulpit Commentary refers to it like being carried as a child upon his father's back. Even as early as when God set up the tribes in the desert to camp around the tabernacle, Benjamin camped in safety with his full blooded brother Joseph's sons Ephraim and Manasseh on the west side of the tabernacle (Numbers 2: 18-22). In Psalms these three tribes are grouped together again, with Benjamin in the middle, "between the shoulders" of his brother tribes. The sons of Joseph took care of their blood brother, Benjamin.

> **Psalm 80:1-2** Give ear, O Shepherd of Israel, You who lead Joseph like a flock; You who dwell *between* the cherubim, shine forth! ² Before Ephraim,

Benjamin, and Manasseh, Stir up Your strength, And come *and* save us!

"Norway (Benjamin) has…excellent relations with the British (Ephraim) and Americans (Manasseh), which one would expect of the descendants of Benjamin…In World War II, Norway fought against the Nazis as allies…Although conquered by Nazi armies, Norway had a vigorous 'underground' which fought the Nazi occupiers."[41]

Iceland and Quebec both have Nordic Benjamite beginnings. Geographically they are both located "between the shoulders" of the two greatest-in-inheritance Israelite nations of the House of Joseph: Ephraim and Manasseh, Britain and the USA respectively.[46] "'Benjamin' therefore is still between 'Ephraim' and 'Manasseh'—between the two mighty 'shoulders' of modern Israel." [46(p.37)]

SUMMARY OF BENJAMIN BEING FOUND

The tribe of Benjamin has been found through their Genesis 49 prophetic description and "wolf" characteristics seen in the Vikings and Normans which settled Norway, Iceland, Northern France, and Quebec, Canada. They still dwell between the shoulders of Ephraim and Manasseh as the Lord described. (See map on next page.)

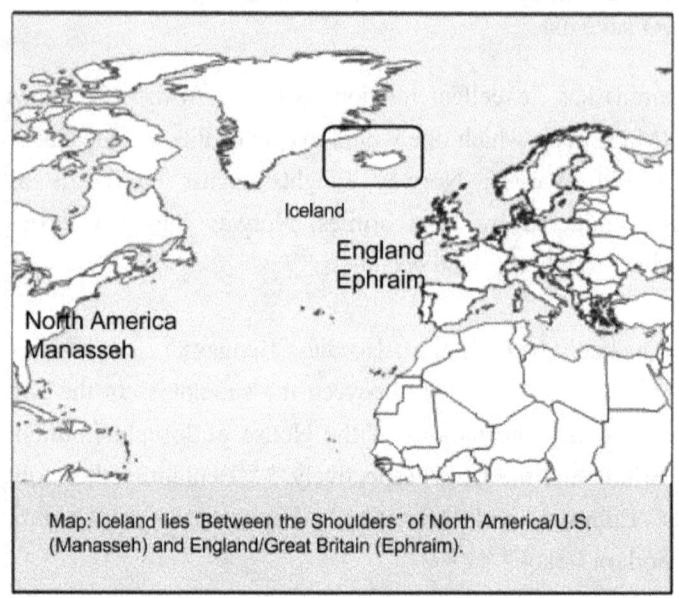

Map: Iceland lies "Between the Shoulders" of North America/U.S. (Manasseh) and England/Great Britain (Ephraim).

MAP 7: ICELAND "BETWEEN THE SHOULDERS."

Note: Benjamin still dwells between the shoulders of Ephraim (Great Britian) and Manasseh (the United States) in their Iceland location.

7

NAPHTALI AND ASHER

Naphtali Found in Sweden and Norway

Naphtali was Jacob's sixth son, (second of Rachel's servant Bilhah) and was a full blood brother to Dan. Named by Rachel, Naphtali's name means "my wrestling" in Hebrew, alluding to her struggle with Leah for superiority in the strange marriage-concubine-child bearing relationship shared among the five of them. Naphtali's lifetime was somewhat unremarkable.

At Jacob/Israel's death, his blessing and prophetic description of Naphtali is short.

> **Genesis 49:21** "Naphtali *is* a deer let loose; He uses beautiful words.

Other words sometimes translated for *deer* are hind or gazelle. Appropriately, a gazelle is the symbol by which the tribe of Naphtali identifies herself. When camping in the desert around the Tabernacle, Naphtali set up on the north side with Asher and Dan (Numbers 2:29-31) under the leadership of Dan. Interestingly, these three tribes became the three sea-faring tribes of Israel, Dan being the leader. They began to explore and spread west earliest on in Israel's Promised Land existence.

This gazelle that Jacob speaks of is not hunted, but "let loose." This word-picture of a hind/deer set loose is found elsewhere in scripture, most outstanding is Habakkuk 3:19, "The LORD God is my strength; He will make my feet like deer's feet, And He will make me walk on my high hills." Salemi quotes K&D Commentary, saying this "hind or gazelle is a simile of a warrior who is skillful and swift in his movements (2Sa 2:18; 1Ch 12:8, cf. Ps 18:33; Hab 3:19). ...here [it] is neither hunted, nor stretched out or grown slim; *but let loose, running freely about* (Job 39:5).[47](brackets mine, emphasis his) Therefore when we go to look for Naphtali among the nations, we should look for warriors who are skilful, agile and running about freely wherever they wish to go.

MOSES' PROPHECY

Moses describes Naphtali in the last days. This ends up being prophetically fulfilled twice.

> **Deuteronomy 33:23** "O Naphtali, satisfied with favor,
> And full of the blessing of the LORD, Possess the west
> and the south."

The first fulfillment of this prophecy came when the tribe of Naphtali received their tribal inheritance in the Promised Land; the second when receiving a nation as their inheritance in the last days. Both times Naphtali is found living in the west and north, making excursions into the land south of them to possess it.

BOUNDARIES OF INHERITANCE

Joshua 19:32-39 gives the descriptions of the town names where Naphtali was to settle. They are located in the north of the Promised Land (see map of Inheritance on page 28), north of Issachar and Zebulon, and in the west Asher's land was Naphtali's boundary. Part of Dan also resettled in this northern region. Notice that again Dan, Issachar and Naphtali are dwelling together as they did in the wilderness.

Assyrian Captivity

When the Assyrians came in the first wave, Naphtali was taken captive as a whole tribe to the east (again, in a position to need to make their way west to possess it later).

> **II Kings 15:29** In the days of Pekah king of Israel, Tiglath-Pileser king of Assyria came and took Ijon, Abel Beth Maachah, Janoah, Kedesh, Hazor, Gilead, and Galilee, <u>all the land of Naphtali; and he carried them captive to Assyria.</u>

Being taken all together makes tracing this tribe one of the easiest trails to follow because they didn't lose their name or get fractured in the process. There is an historical group found to live in the exact area of Assyrian Empire, between the Black and Caspian Seas, at the same time Naphtali was carried away captive from 10-Israel.[47] They are called *Ephthalites*. Salemi[47] came across an interesting footnote in *Encyclopedia Britannica* while researching these Ephthalites.

> *Britannica* also says they are called the "Nephthalites." But then they add that it (i)s a "clerical error." Yet...no *support for that* (clerical error) *claim is given*. Why? Is it because they do not want people to be interested to know where the lost ten tribes are? In doing so draws attention and interest in the Bible? The similarity between the "Nephthalites" and "Naphtali" is glaringly obvious![47(para 9)]

A sixth century AD historian named Procopius who was born in Caesarea, Palestine (now Israel) says that the Ephthalitae Huns are called White Huns, but they separated themselves from other Huns even in their location living away from the "other" Huns. The Ephthalitae Huns' "territory lies immediately to the north of Persia [...] They are not nomads like the other Hunnic peoples, but for a long period have been established in a goodly land." (Procopius, *History of the Wars*. Book I, Ch. III, "The Persian War").[48(para 14)] These White Huns had fair complexions, lived under a single king with a constitution, and they "behaved justly towards neighboring states."[47]

Huns Moving West

Yair Dividiy, historian and founder of BritAm, has traced the bulk of the tribe of Naphtali, as the White Huns, making their way westward before 450 BC. They made it as far west as present-day Norway and Sweden where they began to be referred to as *Hephtalitesas* (or Huns of Naphtali).[47, 50] They remained with close ties and proximity to the tribe of Dan.

> From east Scythia the Naphtali migrated to Norway and the Danes to Denmark. This was proven by Scandinavian tradition, by tracing names, by demographic considerations, and by archaeological finds. The sons of Naphtali were Jahzeel, Guni, Jezer, and Shillem and these appellations are reminiscent of Scandinavian place and ethnic names such as Zealand, Egan, Vraesan, and Sillund.[48(p.240)]

Vikings

Once in Scandinavia, these Naphtali Huns became known as the Vikings, especially of Norway, but also Sweden.[50] More and more people kept coming to this area of Scandinavia, Norway, Sweden, Denmark, Finland

> The influx of population into Scandinavia seems to have been continuous and by the 700's (AD) Scandinavia appears to have become overpopulated. Consequently, the excess "Vikings" of Sweden, Norway, and Denmark began their oversea excursions which led to settlement in Ireland, England, Scotland, France, and elsewhere.[50(para 9)]

Remember the description of Naphtali in the latter days given by Jacob? He calls them a skilful warrior who roves about wherever he wants. Doesn't that sound exactly like the Vikings? And with the sea-faring background of the Naphtali, and their close ties with Asher (Belgium) and Dan (Denmark), it makes perfect sense.

"The Vikings built *swift*, easily maneuverable vessels for their many expeditions, and were skilled navigators across the open seas" (The Viking Age, Norway.org). The Vikings were skillful warriors often plundering, and discovering lands for settlements, and to be mercenaries for other nations as well. [47]

The land of Norway was also called Thul in Old English literature and on ancient maps. Interestingly, *Thul* means "speaker." Remember the second half of Jacob's prophecy about Naphtali? "He uses beautiful words." This also seems a clue toward Norway's Norsemen and the Vikings being Naphtali.[47]

SWEDEN AND NORWAY ARE ONE & RELATED IN ISRAEL

Three different times throughout history Sweden and Norway have been united as one nation, in the 1300's, 1400's and almost all of the 1800's.[47] They had their own "independent laws, parliament, government, administration, church, army, and currency. However, the king mostly resided in Stockholm. Swedes were initially viceroys in Norway."[47 para 1] Why do they keep coming together? Perhaps their hearts know they are from the same tribe, Naphtali.

BEAUTIFUL WORDS

The second half of the Genesis 49 prophecy needs more emphasis for us to believe that Naphtali is found in Sweden and Norway. This phrase "beautiful words" could also mean beautiful speeches or sayings, perhaps even writing. Some of the best writing in the English language comes out of Britain. It would be interesting to discover if those writers have Scandinavian heritage, thus their writings would be a fulfillment to the prophecy. It is not too far a stretch since the Vikings were all over the British Isles in their heyday. However, are there any unambiguous beautiful speeches or words that are attributable to Norway and Sweden? As a matter of fact, yes. Naphtali, in the countries of

> Sweden and Norway sponsors the annual Nobel Prizes, which are "beautiful speeches" or "pleasing

pronouncements" given to noteworthy achievers in a variety of fields. These awards are world-famous and are reported in the world's media every year. No other nations of Europe are so closely identified with the practice of making internationally famous awards to the rest of the world on an annual basis.[47(para 26)]

SUMMARY OF NAPHTALI BEING SWEDEN AND NORWAY

Naphtali is easy to trace from their being exiled in one group whose name for a thousand years didn't change (except that N being dropped "clerically" recently). Their current location in the west of Europe, though fully in the northland, strangely corresponds with their tribal inheritance location within Israel. Naphtali is still living along side Dan and Asher as they did in the desert around the Tabernacle and they give annual beautiful speeches to the world.

תא

ASHER CAN BE FOUND IN
BELGIUM, LUXEMBURG, & SOUTH AFRICA

Asher has been associated by different researchers with different countries such as France or Austria, but with little true evidence. More evidence through prophetic fulfillments in the last days and historical migrations give clues that point more toward Asher being in present day Luxemburg, Belgium and South Africa.

NAME MEANING AND ASHER QUALITIES

Asher was Jacob's eighth son, the second from Leah's maid Zilpah (Genesis 30:12-13). "Leah said, 'I am happy, for the daughters will call me blessed.' So she named him Asher." Asher means happy.

Naphtali and Asher

Prophetic Words and Blessings

Jacob's blessing and last days revelation about his son Asher is short and sweet, but from it we will search for clues to Asher's modern populace.

> **Genesis 49:20** "Bread from Asher *shall be* rich, And he shall yield royal dainties."

Let's break these words down into meaningful clues we can use. Bread, can refer to sustenance of life, either Asher's life or others' lives. While bread may represent actual food, it can also be referring to "economy" or "gain"[51] as seen with its pairing of the word "riches" in this first clause. "Bread <u>from</u> Asher" designates exports, or Asher exporting their gain, which means they have more than enough (again referring to riches). The economy or bread "shall be rich" designating fullness, quality, and deserving of praise, and more than enough for themselves.

"Yield" in the next clause can refer to "give" as in when a tree *yields* fruit.[51] But what about "royal dainties"? Well *royal* seems obvious enough: people of royalty, ruling class or ruling dynasty. *Dainties* perhaps refers to the things that Royals like, the things that please them or make them happy. What substance would please a king? What gift does a visitor bring to a king but gold and jewels, or as in Solomon's day, spices (from the Queen of Sheba).

So if we put this all together, Asher will be a rich exporter with a great economy and provide gold (and other precious metals) and diamonds (and other precious stones) to royal families or to the rich.

The last blessing upon Asher from Moses yields a bit more information about what we should look for.

> **Deuteronomy 33:24-25** And of Asher he said: "Asher *is* most blessed of sons; Let him be favored by his brothers, And let him dip his foot in oil. [25] Your sandals *shall be* iron and bronze; As your days, *so shall* your strength *be*.

Asher will be the <u>most blessed</u> (richest) of Jacob's sons. If Moses was blessing Asher to be favored by his brothers, this hints that Asher was rejected, not favored, and needed a blessing to walk in favor among them.[51]

In this day and age, one might think that if a tribe was prophesied to be the richest and to "dip their foot in oil" they might find a large underground reservoir(s) of oil or petroleum. However, that's not the case. The Hebrew word used here for oil is "shemen."[51,52] It means olive oil which is valuable in caring for the body medically and cosmetically and preparing food. Oil is generally considered valuable. "This was a symbol of affluence and the tribe of Asher was blessed with a promise of affluence to be symbolized by dipping their feet in (olive) oil."[51(para 11)] Particularly, bathing *feet* in oil speaks to the extravagance of riches that will be present in Asher.

"Your sandals shall be iron and bronze." When the word "sandals" is used immediately after talking about a foot dipped in oil referring to wealth and high value commodities that bring wealth, we should look for the *foundation* of that wealth to be in the areas of iron and bronze/brass, high value metals, or mines of these metals that will be present for exporting that will build wealth for Asher in the last days.

DOUBLE MEANING OF "AS YOUR DAYS, SO SHALL YOUR STRENGTH BE"

This phrase meaning could be as simple as Asher will have strength for all his days of life (i.e. they will not die out old and feeble, or they will have grace for every trial sent their way).[51] The whole English sentiment is only two words long in Hebrew. There is no question as to the first word: *ucheyameycha* means "as your days"[52] The second word, *dobecha*, is not found anywhere else in scripture. When the Septuagint was compiled, the un-cross-referenced word was translated "strength...and most of the versions have followed them; but others have rendered it affliction, old age, fame, weakness."[52(para 18)] It could also refer to the riches associated with Asher: "for all your days, so shall your riches last."

The second meaning after we search for the root word (daba) can be found as "rest" or "quietness."[51] The phrase would then mean that for all Asher's days (of enduring difficulty) they will find rest. When examining the location of Asher's land inheritance this meaning is equally plausible. Asher settled the land right up to Israel's northern border (present day Lebanon and Syria) and on the west, they had a long stretch of coastland they had to defend from invaders, pillagers and mauraders.[51]

ASHER'S CHILDREN'S NAMES

> **Genesis 46:17** The sons of Asher *were* Jimnah, Ishuah, Isui, Beriah, and Serah, their sister. And the sons of Beriah *were* Heber and Malchiel.

INHERITANCE IN THE LAND

> **Joshua 19: 24-31** The land allotted to Asher included the cities of Tyre and Zidon. There were 22 total towns and their surrounding villages.

The book of Judges describes how Asher dealt with the people already living in their towns.

> **Judges 1:31-32** Nor did Asher drive out those living in Akko or Sidon or Ahlab or Akzib or Helbah or Aphek or Rehob. [32] The Asherites lived among the Canaanite inhabitants of the land because they did not drive them out.

Even though Asher didn't drive out the Canaanites in their land, they were clearly the dominant or ruling people living in these towns and cities.[51] Remember that the main industry in Tyre and Sidon (the two main Asherite cities) is sea faring pursuits. Asherites learned this trade from those living among them. As happens over the years, the people living in a particular city begin being called after the name of that city; the Israelites (predominately Asherites) living in Sidon began being called Sidonians, those living in Tyre, Tyrians. "Sidonians" ended up being much longer lasting than "Tyrians."[51]

ASHER DURING DAVID'S AND SOLOMON'S REIGNS

Asher was already sending out ships into the western Mediterranean with Dan during the time of the judges of Israel. By David and Solomon's reign they were already mining in the British Isles.[51]

> William Camden, a British historian who lived between 1551 to 1623 states in his work *Britannia*, that, "The merchants of Asher worked the mines of Cornwall, not as slaves, but as masters and exporters" (*Traditions of Glastonbury*, p.28, Capt). Sir Edmund Creasy says that these "mines mainly supplied the glorious adornment of Solomon's Temple" (ibid, p.28). So early on we see from history that the Asherites were already in the mining and exploration business.[51(para Colony of Asher)]

Asher was beginning the first stages of walking in the fulfillment of the prophecies Jacob and Moses spoke over them as they mined in the British Isles during the days of David and Solomon, but that time was not the *fullness* of the prophecy that would show itself in the latter days.

DURING THE ASSYRIAN INVASION

Davidiy describes in *The Tribes*[45] that some of Asher was taken captive to the east by the Assyrians with their 10-Israel brothers (2 Kings 15:29; I Chronicles 5:26;), but it was at this time (700's BC) that the people of Tyre left. "It was the oppressive Assyrian rule that caused many of the Tyrians to leave their city and go found their 'New Town'... Carthage."[51(para 3 'Assyrain Invasion')]

Evidence from the language mix of Phoenician and Hebrew shows that the "'AS' in Phoenician-Hebrew was a shortened form for ASHER...[and] it appears to have been the dialect employed by the northern ten tribes prior to exile."[45(p.276)] It was after the Assyrian invasion and initial imposed exile that portions of Asher made their way north toward the Black Sea region and became a tribe among the others called Cimmerians (spelled Samarians back in 10-Israel, except of course, it was in Hebrew, so our English version is just two phonetic spellings using English letters of the same people), and those who went south to Carthage were referred to as Phoenician (by the people who gave us the written record of the Greco-Romans).

> Ancient Assyrian tablets show that the Assyrians called the Israelites the Bit Khumri. It is this name that reveals the Israelites as the Cimmerians. The Scythians are known as the same race as the Cimmerians, also called the "Sacae" "Beth-Saac," House of Isaac.[51]

The Cimmerians also were known as Scythians (from the *Sacae*) a powerful empire named after the House of Isaac, just as prophesied and as we studied earlier.

ASHER AFTER SCYTHIA

The tribe of Asher, while living among the Scythians, were called Issedones,[51] and they moved into Europe, first Germany and Scandinavia and then into "Holland, France Belgium, Switzerland, and the British Isles, as well as in smaller numbers to other European states."[45(p.270-271)] Interestingly, "in Medieval times Northern Gaul and Belgium was called 'Sidon'."[45(p.333)] That sounds familiar and related to Asher. Also in western Belgium we find the first century BC tribe of Suessiones or Issedones[51] who were conquered by Julius Caesar. The Suessiones were located near the present day Belgium city of Soissons.[53] These names are based on the name "Sidonians" who we know are the tribe of Asher in exile. Another couple of Hebrew links in Belgium are the "Eburones" (based on the name *Eber* which was translated *Hebrews* in English) and the *Menapii* which was formed from *Mna* which became Mnappi or Menapi over time. First Chronicles 7:30 shows Imnah as a major branch (son) of Asher. It means "good fortune."[51] Over time the first "Y" or "I" sound was dropped (the same way it was with Yisrael) becoming Mna.[51] The Eburones and Menapii were large tribes controlling the north regions of Belgium.

Next door, to the southeast of Belgium is the modern country of Luxembourg. They are also descended from Asher as can be seen in their tribal ancestry names: from the Belgic peoples "Treveri, the Ligurians" The Ligurian "tribes were the Boreoi [Boers], the Omani, and the Hessi. These names (are) similar to the sons of Asher" [45 (p.276)] which are found in I Chronicles 7:30. It's unmistakable that Belgium and Luxembourg have the Asherite name written on them. But do these people's characteristics fulfill the prophecies?

Fulfilling the Prophecies

We determined earlier that the prophecies of Jacob and Moses would have us look for Asher among peoples in the latter days who were wealthy, exporters of gold and diamonds, and miners of metals. Luxembourg has the world's highest GDP and an advanced economy that was based on iron and steel mining and production until the 1960's and it is now dominated by banking[54] (which is what you do if you're rich, I suppose.). They have especially close ties with Belgium and the Netherlands.

During the 17th century the Dutch and Belgians joined in the United Kingdom of Netherlands and colonized the Belgian Congo and South Africa where mining of diamonds makes up most of the world's supply. South Africa supplies diamonds and gold, the "dainties of royalty" just as prophesied by Jacob!

> Belgians also settled in South Africa as Boers, Afrikaneers or Dutch. It is interesting that 80% of the world gold, 76% of its chrome, 96% of its platinum, 80% of its manganese and vanadium, and about 45% of its uranium are produced in South Africa.[51(para 19 Assyrian Invasion)]

These diamonds of South Africa are processed in Belgium today. The diamonds mined in the Congo (which is now a "free" republic after Belgium pulled out in 1960) are known as "blood diamonds" because of the conflict associated with that country now.

In a surprising move such as only God can do, South Africa was taken over by the British which looked like it would upset the prophecy of Asher's wealth and mining. However, the inhabitants of north Britain "were Anglo-Brigantian, and Beriah the son of Asher was found in the Brigantes." [49(p.328, 338)] South Africa was settled by men who had lived in the north of Britain.[49] They were men from the tribe of Asher! Related to the people of Belgium, the Boers, they were taking over for.

Another part of the prophecy of Moses was "let him be acceptable to his brethren." South Africa fulfills this as well, just in the negative. Because of the Apartheid policies, of all "western democracies, South Africa has been criticized the most."[51(para 22 Assyrain Invasion)] South Africa needs the blessing of being accepted by his brothers.

ZULU STORY OF SOUTH AFRICA[51]

There is a great story of God coming through miraculously for the people of South Africa when they turned to Him. God promised He would do this.

> **Leviticus 26:8** "And five of you shall chase an hundred, and an hundred of you shall put ten thousand to flight: and your enemies shall fall before you by the sword."

In 1838, there was a massacre of 300 women by the fierce and ungodly Zulu tribe migrating into South Africa. This raiding and pillaging had happened to Asher before, when they lived in Israel, but when they were submitted to God and crying out to Him for help, they received rest from Him. The Voortrekkers in South Africa saw that they would not be able to make peace with the Zulu. Their leader a godly man named Sarel Cilliers, along with 536 armed men, made a covenant with God for help. On December 15, 1838, Cilliers said, "Here we stand today before a holy God of heaven and earth. But we promise Him that if He will give us the victory in the slaughter tomorrow, we will dedicate that day—the l6th of December — to be a holy Sabbath for us and our children unto all future generations."[51(para 23)] It is now known as the Day of the Vow. And on December 16th, when 15,000 Zulu descended on the 536 covenant makers, (after a freaky moment when their gun powder was too wet with dew to fire, but it dried out after they cried to God for mercy) only three trekkers were lightly wounded, none died, but thousands of Zulu died. So many Zulu died that day that the river is now called Blood River. This day is still set apart as a Sabbath in South Africa. Not as a day when the Whites overcame the Blacks, but as a day the Christian civilization who happened to be Caucasian was saved miraculously. The Calvinists from the tribe of Asher then set up a temple to honor God and built a seminary at the former Zulu headquarters to share the gospel with the tribes who had tried to kill them!

SUMMARY OF ASHER

Asher is found in Belgium, Luxembourg and South Africa as they each have traces of the 10-Israel tribe written on their regions and in their latter day traits of exporting, mining and wealth.

8

ISSACHAR AND ZEBULON

TRIBE OF ISSACHAR IS
WESTERN RUSSIA (TULA) AND FINLAND+

BACKGROUND
Issachar was the ninth son of Jacob, and his fifth with Leah (Genesis 30:18). His name means "man of hire" with the accompanying connotation of anything to do with receiving wages.[70] When in the wilderness for 40 years, the tribe of Issachar (54,400 men of war age, plus their families) camped to the east of the Tabernacle with Zebulon under the leadership standard of Judah (Numbers 1:28; 2: 3-4). They made up one of the larger tribes. By the time of the second census they numbered 64,300 (Num 26:25). The sons of Issachar were Tola, Puvah, Job, and Shimron. (Gen 46:13)

INHERITANCE
When the Promised Land was conquered the tribe of Issachar received their inheritance of land south west from the Sea of Galilee. They were

landlocked among the much larger west Manasseh tribe and Gad, Zebulon and Naphtali. But the land they received was some of the best land in Israel, the very fertile Jezreel Plain where they could excel in farming.

PROPHETIC BLESSINGS

The blessings and latter days prophetic description of Issachar by Jacob and Moses were both short.

> **Genesis 49:14-15 NIV** Issachar is a rawboned (strong) donkey lying down among the sheep pens. (NKJV adds: lying down between two burdens") [15] When he sees how good is his resting place and how pleasant is his land, he will bend his shoulder to the burden and submit to forced labor.
>
> **Deuteronomy 33:18-19 KJV** And of Zebulun he said, Rejoice, Zebulun, in thy going out; and, Issachar, in thy tents. [19] They shall call the people unto the mountain; there they shall offer sacrifices of righteousness: for they shall suck of the abundance of the seas, and of treasures hid in the sand.
>
> **Same Deuteronomy 33:18-19 NIV** May the people of Zebulun prosper in their travels. May the people of Issachar prosper at home in their tents. [19] They summon the people to the mountain to offer proper sacrifices there. They benefit from the riches of the sea and the hidden treasures in the sand.

What descriptions in these blessings can we use to find Issachar in the latter days? The Issacharites will be a people satisfied to stay at home in their own land (opposite of those sea-going Vikings) and to prosper there. They will be a strong people, but not a war-like people. Issachar will work hard in his land, and they will be only quasi-independent as seen in the description of "forced labor." Likely, they will be paying tribute to another, stronger nation around them for that peace in the land that they so admire, perhaps even paying two nations, because of the "two burdens" between which they dwell. They will be located with a seashore from which to benefit from the abundance of its "richness of the seas." They will be ones who call people to the mountain (a reference to Mount Zion perhaps.) and offer good, righteous sacrifices there. "Treasures in their sand" reminds me of Middle Eastern oil, so perhaps this phrase of the prophecy refers to when Issachar returns to dwell in the land of Israel at the end. Alternately, the whole end section of this prophecy could be referring to Zebulon, with the phrase of "Issachar in thy tents" being only a clause, which is the way we will discuss it in the section on Zebulon, next.

Collins states,
> To identify this nation, we must look for a nation in Europe (and likely Scandinavia) which has a tradition of being quasi-independent ("under tribute"), located "between" two stronger nations or spheres of influence (the "two burdens"), and dwelling in reasonable peace and prosperity (their "rest was good, and...the land...was pleasant.")[71(para 12)]

DURING THE PHOENICIAN PERIOD OF DAVID'S & SOLOMON'S REIGNS.

Life progressed normally for the tribe of Issachar in their land, God blessed them with wisdom. The main thing that stands out about Issachar is one verse hidden in the description of David's war at Hebron:

> **I Chronicles 12:32** of the sons of Issachar who had understanding of the times, to know what Israel ought to do, their chiefs were two hundred; and all their brethren were at their command;

According to the *Jewish Encyclopedia of 1906*, Issachar was known for being excellent scholars, especially of the Torah, and also of sciences.[74] They also were "most influential in making proselytes"[74(para 4)] because of their deep study of the Law of Moses. (A modern version of that sentence reads: Issacharites were evangelists and missionaries). Many of their tribe's leaders served on the Sanhedrin to guide Israel throughout the ages.[74] According to Salemi, "Issachar were men of science, law, and of astronomy, (able) to figure out times, dates and seasons for Israel to observe on the calendar made by Issachar."[72]

Wisdom elevated Issachar into a leadership role in Israel, and their teaching of the law and the times of Israel to proselytes abroad would have made a name for them outside of the kingdom of Israel. Therefore it is "logical to assume that the foreigners would have named the entire empire after them"[72(pg 12)] Interestingly, that is actually where the name "Phoenicia" originated, after the fact, of course. The Phoenicians were called the "Puni" or "Phuni"[72] which comes from Issachar's son "Puah, the family of Punites" (Numbers 26:23). (Remember the P and F sounds were interchangeable in these civilizations as we talked about earlier.) The main cities of the Phoenician Empire were Tyre and Sidon on the Mediterranean coast of current day Israel and Lebanon. The Sakkara conquered Sidon for a while.[72] Historian Yair Davidiy (in *Lost Israelite Identity*, 1996) proved the Sakkara to be Israelites. The Sakkara (phonetically: Sac-car-A) actually come from the tribe of Issachar (Phonetically: ISSA--car)—we can hear it in their name—and "the Phoenicians received their name from PUNI -Issachar's son"[72(pg 12)] of the same name.

So while Dan and Asher were out in their ships traveling, Issachar was at home, satisfied in his tents (exactly like the prophecy) to direct the traffic of the empire to where they should go. And it was all based on the wisdom God imparted to them through the Law and their studies and their knowledge and understanding of "what Israel ought to do." They recognized the times and seasons of God's blessing. They sent their brother-tribes to fulfill their destiny. At the same time those brother-tribes brought back shiploads of treasure from the western Mediterranean, Africa and the Americas, and they explored those areas, leaving fledgling colonies that became their eventual salvation from the Assyrians 250 years later, and again and again over the next 1,500 years.

Issachar and Zebulon

God really does have wide-sweeping plans that are bigger than we could ever ask or imagine!

After the Assyrian exile

Issachar went into exile over the 20 year timeframe with their brother tribes. Some went north into Russia, as seen in the name Tula in the city and river there near Moscow in most-west Russia. Continuing on northward, the tribe of Issachar ended their journey of migration in Finland, and became called the Finnish people.

During the Scythian Period of 10-Israel history, a large segment of Issachar can be found in the Zagros Mountains of western Iran. They were called Sagartii or Asakarta.[72] The name of Issachar is still heard in their name *Asakarta*. Ptolemy records in his rendition of history a group called Sagaruce who lived to the east of the Caspian Sea.[72] East of Scythia, Ptolemy also mentions in Serica a people called the *Asmiraea* which in Semitic languages sounds like Issachar's son Shimron. Davidiy records that in Carmania lived a group called the Isatichae. (The Tribes pp57-58) All of these groups go by names derived from Issachar or his sons.

As Scythia began to break apart, Issachar, along with the rest of 10-Israel began to migrate again into the European nations we know today. Davidiy finds that "from Scythia to Sarmatia all of these peoples were to move into, Germany and Scandinavia and from there into Holland, France Belgium, Switzerland, and the British Isles, as well as in smaller numbers to other European states."[45] p.270-271 The groups that made up Issachar landed in Finland.

Issachar is Finland with prophetic fulfillment

Genesis 46:13 names Issachar's sons for us: Tola, Puvah, Job, and Shimron. Each man became a tribal leader. There are also four sub-tribes that make up Finland in its establishment: "The Karelian, Savo, Tavastians, Ostrobothnians."[72] The firstborn, Tola became the Tavastians. Helsinki, the capital of Finland is located in Tavastland. The tribal leadership mantel stayed with the oldest son's descendants.

Incidentally, the ancient capital city of Finland "Turky" was also located in Tavastland.[72] The second-born Phuvah became the Savo people of Finland.[72] Job became the Ostrobothnians, and Shimron the Karelians.[72]

The main prophetic identifications are 1. a strong donkey lying between two burdens 2. a resting place that is good and of pleasant land 3. bend to put his shoulder to work hard and 4. submit to forced labor, which could mean "paying tribute" instead of the immediate connotation in the western mind of slavery.

The Finns are a strong, stubborn people who work hard to produce food from their land, even as frigid and harsh as their winters are. This donkey-symbolized characteristic of stubbornness has made Finland "an agricultural center in Scandinavia."[72] However, they have to "bend their shoulder" with hard work to cause this land to produce fruits and be good pleasant land. Yet still, the Finns are satisfied with the peace of this land and to work hard "in their own tents." Finland has never been a colonizing people; it is not in their God-given nature.

Finland lies between Russia to the east and Scandinavia and greater Europe to the west.

Finland's own Foreign Office self-describes Finland as "a buffer between East and West."[73] This location has caused them problems over the centuries especially when mixed with the (prophesied) personality of this nation of being satisfied to stay at home within their own "tents." The Swedes ruled Finland in the 1700-1800s until a war with Russia led to Russia dominating Finland with dictatorial powers in 1903.[71] These powers literally put Finland "under tribute" to Russia until WWI when the Finns volunteered to fight both for Russia and for Germany (two burdens again).[71] As WWI ended Finland became more and more Scandinavian and European, but with the next world war,

> The Finns made a heroic resistance against the Russians, but had to sign a treaty ceding territory and dominance

to Russia. Finland remained a nation "under tribute." When Germany attacked Russia in 1941, Finland briefly allied itself with Germany before signing an armistice with both Great Britain and Russia in 1944. At the end of World War II, Finland had to pay certain amounts of finished industrial goods (more "tribute") to the Russians.[71(para 14)]

Currently, Finland has become neutral between East and West and lost some of its sovereignty in order to maintain this peace, safety and prosperity that they crave.[71] That "neutrality" is Finland/Issachar's current form of "paying tribute." They are "crouching down" or "resting" between these two burdens rather than fighting them.

SUMMARY OF ISSACHAR
We know Issachar became Finland by following not only the trail of their migration, but also by seeing how they fulfill every word of prophecy given by Jacob and Moses. Even from the mouth of one of their own Finnish heroes, Marshall Mannerheim, in a speech, he once referred to the Finns as being "sons of Issachar"[72, 73] It is their own tradition that places them as descendants of the 10 Lost Tribes of Israel…so I suppose they are not lost after all.

תא

TRIBE OF ZEBULON IS HOLLAND AND THE DUTCH
Zebulon is Jacob's 10th son, his 6th with Leah. His name comes from Leah's sentiment of "God has endowed me with a good gift" (Genesis 30:20) at Zebulon's birth, and it means "glorious dwelling place."[75]

INHERITANCE
The portion of Israel that was given to Zebulon was also landlocked like Issachar, though in the west, just inside Asher from the Mediterranean coast (see map on page 28).

LATTER DAYS PROPHECIES AND BLESSING OF ZEBULON

Genesis 49: 13 "Zebulun shall dwell by the haven of the sea; He *shall become* a haven for ships, And his border shall adjoin Sidon.

HOW DOES HOLLAND FULFILL THIS ANCIENT PROPHECY?

A "haven of the sea" is easily translated as a harbor, a place sheltered from the sea. Holland is quite literally sheltered by their dike system, which keeps the sea from rolling over them. The next prophetic phrase, "haven for ships," indicates that there will also be a port for ships as a major part of their industry and wealth. Until 2002, Rotterdam, Holland was the busiest port in the world. Overtaken by Singapore now, Rotterdam is still the largest in Europe, and fifth in the world (2011) by volume of traffic moving about.[76] The Port of Rotterdam is so large that it actually contains five separate ports and three distribution parks.[76] Not only does it handle traffic from the high seas, but also barge traffic moving throughout the Rhine River waterways. It is the gateway to Europe via canals into the mainland.

The third phrase of the Genesis 49 prophecy takes a little more digging to understand, because it is obvious that Holland does not border Sidon. Sidon is located in current day Lebanon. There is not an easily discernable connection between Lebanon and Holland these days either. Holland is actually known for being kind to the Jews, opposite of the current latter-days' climate of Arab leaders in Lebanon.

Stephen Collins says, "The key may lie in the Hebrew word translated 'border,' which literally means **'thighs.'** This Hebrew word is so translated in Daniel 2:32 in the phrase 'its belly and thighs of brass.'"[77] (p.403) This description of *thighs,* according to Dr Charles Dorothy of Claremont Graduate School, also includes the human pubic area. So the Genesis 49 phrase about Zebulon could be translated: "His thighs and pubic region shall join Sidon." What does that have to do with Holland? Have you heard of Amsterdam's red light district? The capital city of

ISSACHAR AND ZEBULON

Holland is famous for its legal sex trade, both sex shops and prostitution are on full display there. What you may not know is that according to Collins,

> The ancient Sidonians were famous for officially tolerating sinful sex practices which were part of the fertility cult practices of Baal worship. Wicked Queen Jezebel, whose name is synonymous with brazen sexual temptation, was a Sidonian.
>
> Official Dutch tolerance of a major industry in sexual sin parallels the Sidonian tolerance of similar practices, and would give meaning to the Genesis 49 prophecy about modern Zebulon being comparable to the sexually-sinful Sidonians"[77] (p 403-404)

With that explanation of Holland's sex trade, it is simple to see that Holland indeed is the modern nation described in the three phrases of Jacob's ancient Genesis 49 Prophecy.

ANOTHER PROPHECY ABOUT ZEBULON

Moses' prophecy over Zebulon is related to Issachar, but also refers to itself and how Zebulon and Issachar are inter-related.

> **Deuteronomy 33:18-19 (KJV)** "And of Zebulun he said, Rejoice, Zebulun, in thy going out; and, Issachar, in thy tents. [19] They shall call the people unto the mountain; there they shall offer sacrifices of righteousness: for they shall suck of the abundance of the seas, and of treasures hid in the sand.

ABUNDANCE OF THE SEA: FISH AND OIL. Zebulon in Holland has great wealth and a history in the fisheries industry (abundance of the seas) even today. Their unique method of preserving herring with salt saved many families from starvation through hard winters for centuries, especially in the Middle Ages.[78]

Holland's use of their dike systems has literally "sucked" their land from the sea. Beyond that, while drilling for oil, they "discovered a huge 'gas bell' under the northern Netherlands and North Sea."[79 (p.64)] Both the fishing and the gas have added wealth and sustenance to Zebulon in Holland

"TREASURES HID IN SAND:" OIL AND DIAMONDS. The Dutch were once a colonizing nation. Oil-rich Indonesia was once known as the Dutch West Indies. Even when Indonesia gained independence after WWII, Royal Dutch/Shell Oil remained one of the premier oil companies in the world and maintained its name.[78]

Present day South Africa began as a Dutch plantation. Because of 16th and 17th centuries' mixed interests of the Dutch East India Company, combining Protestant missionary work with their fast merchant ships, the bulk of the settlers in South Africa were Dutch Huguenots. As bad a rap as colonization gets today, it was a blessing to South Africa to receive the gospel. Those fast ships were used for transporting diamonds and gold back to Holland. Amsterdam has for centuries now been famous for its diamond cutting industry for the world's diamonds.[78] It is probably not a coincidence that it has been generations of mainly Jewish diamonds workers in Amsterdam who have hand cleaved, divided and set these diamonds.[78] ("Jewish workers" as in the tribe of Judah who have not returned home to the modern state of Israel yet). It is God working out his Word to complete it in these latter days.

ASSYRIAN EXILE
So how did Zebulon end up in Holland? Like the rest of 10-Israel, they were exiled by the Assyrian Army in the 700s BC. They were probably dispersed in the second and third waves, and some left ahead of the army after the first group of tribes were taken captive. Of those who were settled in Assyria, we can find some of their names on ancient maps. Part of Zebulon settled into a kingdom called Zabulistan.[78] This kingdom was located south of Kabul, Afghanistan. The people of Zabulistan, also

associated with Sakastan, evacuated some time before the Muslim Period (a minimum of 1300 years since Mohammad wasn't even born until 570 AD). According to Davidy, Zabulistan was colonized "by the Scythian hero called 'ZOHAK', whose name is actually a variant of ISAAC. Zohak was considered responsible for having settled the *inhabitants of Zabulistan in their places*"[49] (p321) Zebulon rested in this place before joining up with the Cimmerans and Scythians as they made their way into Europe in waves with their brother tribes to settle new areas.

Zebulon's sons were named Sered, and Elon, and Jahleel. Elon is also Helon. (Genesis 46:14, Numbers 10:6) And Helon's son is Eliab (Numbers 2:7) who was the captain of the tribe of Zebulon. These became sub-tribe names of Zebulon, especially Elon and Helon. It is clear to see the modern name of "Holland" in "Helon."[49]

Jumping back to the Iran area where 10-Israel was settled, the name of Zebulon is found in the name "Sabalingoi" (SEB-a-leen-goy) which can be broken into Sabalin-goi. *Goi* simple means "people" in Hebrew and Sabalin is referring to Zebulon with a slightly foreign accent that switches the Z and S sounds.[49] According to Davidiy, "The Sabalingoi lived to the north of the Sigulones (whose name in Hebrew means 'Chosen Ones') and of the Saxons and in turn, to the north of the Sabalingoi were the Chali sons of Jahleel."[49(p.323)] The name *Jaheel* would have been pronounced *Yachlayl* in Hebrew, since all words with a J were adapted from the Y-sound in Hebrew.[78] Jahleel was one of Zebulon's sons. Thus Zebulon's tribe and sub-tribal names appearing in this area of Zebulistan place them in ancient Persia in the same way Dan appears marking the territory of their travels and settlement with their name.

Zebulon moved into Holland among the Saxons (Sac's sons) which we've already established as being named after Isaac, according to the prophecy that 10-Israel would be named after Isaac.

THE WINDMILL OF HOLLAND

A final interesting tidbit connecting Holland to Zebulon is the iconic symbol of Holland, the windmill. It is found all over the country. The name Zebulon is made up of three Hebrew letters, which each have a meaning:

Zayin: "fish-hook or hook"[79]
Bet: "house" or "home/dwelling"
Lamed: "movement, streaming or impulse to action"[79]

This simple meaning of the letters when spelling Zebulon describes a windmill's function. It is a place of dwelling, a home for someone. It hooks up water using the movement of the wind for its energy. The windmill has been engineered and used in Holland since 1200 AD. Its use to move water is exclusively Dutch. And can be traced back to the Medo-Persia era when Zebulon was one of 10-Israel's tribes residing exactly in Persia. Zebulon exported the technology when they migrated, and now if you know Hebrew, the windmill practically screams the connection between modern Holland and ancient Zebulon.[79]

Can we write off all these similarities as simple coincidence? Remember the Hebrew language has no word for coincidence. Everything is planned out by a loving God who enjoys giving clues and insights to those who will search it out.

9

LEVI

We can't leave the tribe of Levi out of our search. We know from biblical sources that most of the Levites stayed attached to Judah and Benjamin in Judea. We also know that parts of the Levites went into exile with 10-Israel and did not return, and parts of Levi went into exile with the kingdom of Judah and returned only in about the same 10% proportion as the rest of Judah.

BACKGROUND

Levi was the third son of Jacob and Leah. His name literally means "attached."

> **Genesis 29:34** She (Leah) conceived again and bore a son, and said, "Now this time my husband will become attached to me, because I have borne him three sons." Therefore his name was called Levi.

God had a lot more in mind for Levi and his descendants down the road than just fulfilling Leah's empty heart concerning her husband. He desired to see the Levites *attached* to Him.

THE PERSONALITY OF LEVI ENDURES

The dominant trait of Levites is their zeal for rightness and the Law of God. Levi was the other brother that went with Simeon to avenge his sister Dinah's honor in Shechem. Through trickery and a sharp sword these two sons of Jacob in their hotheaded zeal put to death the men of an entire town (Genesis 34:25). There was ferocity in Levi that was passed down to his progeny. After the exodus when God was forming Israel into a nation, it was the Levites who stepped forward in the wilderness two different times to show their zeal for God and His law. The first time was after the golden calf incident (discussed below under Inheritance). The second time was recorded in Numbers 25 when Israel was sinning with the daughters of Moab and their idol, Baal of Peor. Israel as a whole had just begun to repent when a certain Simeonite flaunted his sin in front of Israel's leaders. In response, Phinehas ran into the man's tent and thrust a javelin through the man and woman together! That is some major zeal. That zeal stopped the plague of God's wrath against Israel too. This is what God said afterward:

> **Numbers 25: 11-13** "Phinehas the son of Eleazar, the son of Aaron the priest, has turned back My wrath from the children of Israel, because he was zealous with My zeal among them, so that I did not consume the children of Israel in My zeal. [12] Therefore say, 'Behold, I give to him My covenant of peace; [13] and it shall be to him and his descendants after him a covenant of an <u>everlasting priesthood</u>, because he was zealous for his God, and made atonement for the children of Israel.'"

The gift of God to the Levites because of their zeal was the priesthood for eternity. You can never out-give God!

WHAT ELSE DID THE LEVITES DO? As time passed and the priesthood developed among the Levites, three distinct segments of

LEVI

Levites separated themselves in their duties according to the three surviving sons of Aaron: "Gershon, Kohath, and Merari" (Genesis 46:11). Numbers 3:25-37 describes these separated duties. The Meraris were to keep the hard tabernacle frames, and equipment such as tent pegs and poles for the structure of the tabernacle and the courtyard in good repair. The Gershonites' duties included caring for the softer side, the tabernacle tent, the Tent of Meeting, the coverings, ropes etc. The Kohaths' duties were to care for the ark and all the instruments used in worship such as the altar, tables, curtains and so forth, everything that was inside the Tabernacle and Holy of Holies.

> The son of Aaron, Kohath, is where the very common family name "Cohen" is derived. So if you know any Cohens, they are related to Aaron and eligible for the priesthood!

I Chronicles 6 describes Levites as singers, instrument players and worshippers before the Lord. There were so many that David had to arrange a rotation sequence. First Chronicles 9 describes other Levites as guards of the temple and maintenance priests for the implements used in sacrifice or shepherds of the sacrificial flocks for the temple.

INHERITANCE

Levi was not given any land inheritance in the Promised Land, but was given the priesthood. Their inheritance was the Lord Himself! (Joshua 13:33)

> **Numbers 18:21, 23, 24** "Behold, I have given the children of Levi all the tithes in Israel as an inheritance in return for the work which they perform, the work of the tabernacle of meeting... ²³ But the Levites shall perform the work of the tabernacle of meeting, and they shall bear their (Israel's) iniquity; *it shall be* a statute forever, throughout your generations, that among the children of Israel they shall have no inheritance. ²⁴ For the tithes of the children of Israel, which they offer up *as* a heave offering to the LORD, I have given to the Levites

> as an inheritance; therefore I have said to them, 'Among the children of Israel they shall have no inheritance.'"

Levi lived in towns among both Israel and Judah once the split was made. To perform their yearly service in the temple in Jerusalem in later times, the Levite made his way to Jerusalem for his assigned weeks of duty. During both exiles members of the tribe of Levi accompanied Israel and Judah into the nations.

Exodus 32 recounts the first reason Levi was chosen by the Lord as His priests. They were completely loyal to His instructions. After Moses came down Mount Sinai and found the Israelites worshipping the golden calf,

> **Exodus 32:26-29** then Moses stood in the entrance of the camp, and said, "Whoever *is* on the LORD's side—*come* to me!" And all the sons of Levi gathered themselves together to him. ²⁷ And he said to them, "Thus says the LORD God of Israel: 'Let every man put his sword on his side, and go in and out from entrance to entrance throughout the camp, and let every man kill his brother, every man his companion, and every man his neighbor.'" ²⁸ So the sons of Levi did according to the word of Moses. And about three thousand men of the people fell that day. ²⁹ Then Moses said, "Consecrate yourselves today to the LORD, that He may bestow on you a blessing this day, for every man has opposed his son and his brother."

So God chose Levi to minister before Him forever because of this one decision to stand with Him and Moses against their brothers and against "the easy way" of going along with the crowd. Throughout their generations Levi often had to stand against the crowd to honor God's Word.

Peter Salemi writes, "Of course with the history of Levi and his matters to settle this with the sword, it is no wonder that they did it with such zeal. They were also a perfect choice for the task of butchering animals for the sacrifices." 82(para 6)

The easiest way to identify Levi in the nations is by their family name. So when you come across family names derived from Kohath such as Cohen, Cowan, Kohen, or Levi, Levey, or Dunlevi you are meeting one from the tribe of Levi. Of course there are other names too, but those are common here in the States.

JACOB'S & MOSES' PROPHETIC DESCRIPTIONS OF LEVI

> **Genesis 49:5-7** Levi *are* brothers; Instruments of cruelty *are in* their dwelling place. ⁶ Let not my soul enter their council; Let not my honor be united to their assembly; For in their anger they slew a man, And in their self-will they hamstrung an ox. ⁷ Cursed *be* their anger, for *it is* fierce; And their wrath, for it is cruel! I will divide them in Jacob And scatter them in Israel.

The above description Jacob gives is not a nice one for Levi's future. He calls them instruments of cruelty; he curses their fierce anger and wrath. He promises that they will be divided and scattered in Israel. And they were.

> **Deuteronomy 33:8-11** And of Levi he said: "*Let* Your Thummim and Your Urim *be* with Your holy one, Whom You tested at Massah, And with whom You contended at the waters of Meribah, ⁹ Who says of his father and mother, 'I have not seen them'; Nor did he acknowledge his brothers, Or know his own children; For they have observed Your word And kept Your covenant. ¹⁰ They shall teach Jacob Your judgments, And Israel Your law. They shall put incense before You, And a whole burnt sacrifice on Your altar.
> ¹¹ Bless his substance, LORD, And accept the work of his hands; Strike the loins of those who rise against him, And of those who hate him, that they rise not again."

Moses' blessing of the tribe of Levi (of whom he was one, I should probably point out) is a little less severe. Moses softens toward his kinsmen, and remember, Moses talks to God like a friend would. Here Moses seems to be reminding God of the good that has come out of Levi through the desert wandering time. Levi has taught the law and judgments of God to Israel and observed them. They have burned incense and sacrifices before the Lord. Moses asks God to bless Levi's substance and to accept his work and to strike down any who come against him or hates him.

Interestingly, from this first phrase of the prophecy we see the *Thummim* and *Urim*. We know historically and biblically that these are the two stones kept by the High Priest to determine God's will in matters of Israel (Exodus 28: 29-30). But their names mean "lights" and "perfections" respectively. In this prophecy when Moses says to God of Levi's tribe, "*Let* Your Thummim and Your Urim *be* with Your holy one," he is asking that the Levitical priests be blessed with the light of God's truth and that God's perfections might shine through them and their actions.

Second Chronicles 30:25 alludes that many of the Levites who fled the Assyrians went south into Judah. But not all of them. Part of Levi went into exile with 10-Israel in the 700's BC and did not return, and most went out with Judah in 586 BC and only partially returned. The Levites who returned to Judea then rebuilt their numbers went into exile again with the remnant of the Jews in 70 AD, and we should expect to find them scattered among 10-Israel and the Jews today. Many members of the tribe of Levi today know who they are, but they are of the group who left with Judah in their exiles of 586 BC and/or 70 AD. The original Levites scattered among 10-Israel are the ones we are searching for in this research.

LEVI AMONG THE SCOTS

There are some who believe that the Scots may be a major contingent of the tribe of Levi.[80] They base their ideas on several bits of evidence including the ferocity with which the Scotsmen have fought throughout their history, primarily those from the Scottish Highlands. Even in the 20th century, the most noble fighters in some of the most difficult jobs have come from among the Highlanders. They are the ones chosen to guard the Queen of England! No wonder too. Their fierce and loyal fighting comes from deep inside; it is part of who God made them to be from back with their ancestor Levi, son of Jacob. And they guarded the tabernacle and temple in Jerusalem with that same effort.

OLD TESTAMENT FOOD LAWS are found within the culture of Scotland which is not surprising since of all the tribes of Israel, Levi would be the one most likely to cling to the law even in a new surrounding. They were great proponents of God's laws. John Toland describes a Scottish "aversion to pork and black pudding" in his 1714 book *Reasons for Naturalising the Jews in Great Britain and Ireland.*[80]

"PASTORS AND TEACHERS OF THE LAW" is how Levi is described in Deuteronomy 33:9-10 (see page 139). Many Scottish people who have in the last 200 years left Scotland to become again, "scattered among the Israelites" have been preachers, pastors, teachers, professors and biblical scholars.[80] Robert A Peterson, a professor of Systematic Theology at Covenant Theological Seminary in St. Louis, Missouri said, "Scotland has probably produced more missionaries in proportion to her population than any other nation on earth."[80] Davidiy says, "The Scots were once noted for theological hairsplitting and philosophizing-like many Talmudically trained Jews."[49] (p.294) Levi is fulfilling their God-given destiny in exile, just like the other tribes are.

THERE IS AN UNUSUAL & PARTICULAR MUSICAL INSTRUMENT associated with the Levites and their worship in Psalms 15:16 and 28. It is called a psaltry. Strong's Concordance gives 5035 as a reference number for psaltry, and it is described as "nebel {nay'-bel}; from 'nabel' (5034); a skin-bag for liquids (from collapsing when empty); hence, a vase (as similar in shape when full); also a lyre (as having a body of like form):--bottle, pitcher, psaltery, vessel, viol."[81] A skin bag or bladder that produces music? There is only one instrument in the world that comes to mind with that description: bagpipes. And where are they most prevalent? Scotland. A simple coincidence? Perhaps it is a deep connection with worship and their Levitical heritage.

CURRENT DNA TESTING AVAILABLE[82]

Just for your knowledge, whether or not a person is Jewish is established by the mother's heritage, but it is the father's bloodline that determines the *tribe* of Israel to which a person belongs. This traceability is particularly useful in light of DNA testing available only in recent years.

Because it would take too much time to explain all the ins and outs of DNA, I point you toward this source to get you started: http://creationists.org/patrickyoung/article12.html if you want to dig out the details of how the following statement is possible: Self-identified Cohanim* from all over the globe, raised by families for generation upon generation in different worlds separated from one another, all carry the same identifiable gene, in their Y chromosome, that is traceable to a common ancestor from approximately 3,000 years ago.[82] We know that ancestor by the name Aaron.

Interestingly, men who identified themselves as only from the tribe of Levi, not of the line of Aaron, showed wholly different sets of haplotypes as compared to the Cohanim.[82] And Jews in general (those we know of currently, who are from the tribe of Judah), while the DNA shows similarities, it is not in the same gene areas that the Cohanim share.[82] The

---

* Cohanim means from the tribe of Levi and the line of Aaron, therefore they are eligible to serve as a high priest of Israel.

high priests' family line has succeeded in keeping pure from father to son for thousands of years now.[82]

What makes this purity of identifiable high priest line so interesting is that in Exodus (twice) and Numbers God promises that this privileged calling of the priesthood, serving between God and the people was an eternal calling.

> **Exodus 40:15** You shall anoint them, as you anointed their father, that they may minister to Me as priests; for their anointing shall surely be an everlasting priesthood throughout their generations.

> **Romans 11:29** For the gifts and the calling of God *are* irrevocable.

When worship is restored between the New Nation of Israel and Yahweh, the priestly role will also be restored to the cohanim among the tribe of Levi.

Zechariah prophesied in 12:10-14 that when Christ is revealed, Levi (and other tribes) will mourn and repent. Levi will be restored to God first (Malachi 3:2-4) and they will draw Israel back to Him through the radical personality He created in them and the ways in which they cling to God's Word with ferocity. Among those Cohanim will be men that left Israel with 10-Israel in the three waves in the 700's BC and never returned. There will be Cohen men from former Persia (Iran), and Alexandria, Egypt, from Scandinavia and Europe, from the United States and the British Commonwealth including the "ends of the earth" in Australia and New Zealand; Cohanim will flock from everyplace in the earth that 10-Israel and the Jews were scattered, and they will lead the way back to Mount Zion with shouts of joy! Mount Zion is both the literal mountain of Zion upon which the city of Jerusalem is currently built (and was in the past), and Mount Zion is also is a biblical euphemism for dwelling with God in the way He desires. Thank God for fulfilled destiny!

> **Malachi 3:3-4** He will sit as a refiner and a purifier of silver; <u>He will purify the sons of Levi</u>, And purge them as gold and silver, That they may offer to the LORD An offering in righteousness. <u>Then the offering of Judah and Jerusalem</u> Will be pleasant to the LORD, As in the days of old, As in former years.

Zacharias, himself a Cohan Levite, prophesied and prayed blessing over his son John (the Baptist) that John and the sons of Levi:

> **Luke 1:74-75** To grant us that we, Being delivered from the hand of our enemies, Might serve Him without fear, [75] In holiness and righteousness before Him all the days of our life.

David prophesied in Psalms that God's resting place would be in Zion.

> **Psalms 132:13-14** For the LORD has chosen Zion; He has desired *it* for His dwelling place: [14] "This *is* My resting place forever; Here I will dwell, for I have desired it.

Amos prophesied that the tabernacle of David would be restored. Not Solomon's temple of grandeur or Moses' Tent of Meeting, but David's tabernacle!

> **Amos 9:10-11** On that day I will raise up The tabernacle of David, which has fallen down, And repair its damages; I will raise up its ruins, And rebuild it as in the days of old; [12] That they may possess the remnant of Edom, And all the Gentiles who are called by My name," Says the LORD who does this thing.

"David's Tabernacle" refers to worship.

Amos's prophecy is quoted in Acts 16:15-18, as if they are still looking for it's fulfillment, discounting any thought that Herod's Temple could be its fulfillment. David's tabernacle was one of worship and prayer—24/7 worship and prayer—led by the Levites, and all Israel participated. But look at the reason Amos quotes for this restoration of David's worship house for Yahweh in verse 12: Worship will arise from Zion to capture the Gentiles called by His name. Who are Gentiles called by God's name? (Christ) It's the Christians He is after! Someone else is mentioned here too, before the Gentiles called by God's name. The "remnant of Edom." Who is that?

REMNANT OF EDOM

The modern day country located in ancient Edom is Jordan.

Jordan... as in Islam!

Collins describes also that "One dominant nation of the Edomites was the nation of "Teman," whose name was preserved in the "Ottoman" Empire, the precursor of the modern nation of Turkey."[86(para 3 in reply)] The Christian Byzantine Empire was conquered by the Ottoman Empire (1299-1922) and was enslaved in Islam, as is modern-day Turkey, Lebanon, Syria and Jordan who were once part of the Ottoman Empire. The descendants of the Ottomans are part of the remnant of Edom!

Can you imagine a dream of God that is so big that He might mean that He wants to redeem and restore to His house of worship and prayer those enslaved to Islam? How is that even possible? First, nothing is impossible with God (Luke 1:37). Second, the Edomites are also sons of Abraham through Ishmael. Third, practically how could redemption come to a religion that is already the most prayer-oriented religion in the world (They pray five times a day.) except a greater prayer movement come along? One that prays 24/7! One under the unction and restorative power of the Almighty. One that comes from Mount Zion. That is how the Lord can redeem the remnant of Edom!

IHOP: International Houses of Prayer—not pancakes

The Lord is already at work to raise up this prayer and worship movement in other parts of the world through Houses of Prayer, Prayer Furnaces etc. that keep the fire of worship and prayer burning 24/7. I have gotten to personally visit eight of them and lead worship in three of them so far. There are at least four already functioning in Jerusalem today! But there is coming a day when the main one will be in Jerusalem and it will be led by the Levites.

> **Zechariah 12:7** "The LORD will save the tents of Judah first, so that the glory of the house of David and the glory of the inhabitants of Jerusalem shall not become greater than that of Judah.

Zechariah prophesied nearly 600 years before Judea was scattered in 70 AD that the tribe of Judah would be the first to return. This has already been fulfilled in the formation of the modern State of Israel. It is made up primarily of the tribe of Judah. The next step is the identification and revival of Levi so that God's voice through them may call back their brothers from every corner of the earth.

Levi's role after Jesus' final sacrifice

The whole chapter of Hebrews 7 discusses the need for a new high priest, namely Yeshua. And there is a changing of the Levites' role among Israel because Jesus became the final and complete sacrifice for sin. Levi's animal sacrifice role is now finished. Before Jesus the daily sacrifices and sin sacrifices pointed to the One who was coming to be the complete sacrifice forever and always.

> **Hebrews 7:18-19** For on the one hand there is an annulling of the former commandment because of its weakness and unprofitableness, [19] for the law made nothing perfect; on the other hand, *there is the* bringing in of a better hope, through which we draw near to God.

However, sacrifice is not Levi's only role. Would God give Himself as a tribe's only inheritance and then do away with it? No. Just as the other 12 tribes of Israel have had their land restored (though only Judah is occupying currently) as part of the fulfillment of God's promise to restore them in the last days, He will restore the Levites to a redeemed role and inheritance among Israel.

The Levites' guardianship and protection of the Word of Yahweh is now being restored.[83] Some may see this as legalistic or even heresy, but God Himself says through Jeremiah that the Levitical role will continue through eternity in the very same breath as he prophesies Yeshua on David's throne!

> **Jeremiah 33:20-22** Thus says the LORD: 'If you can break My covenant with the day and My covenant with the night, so that there will not be day and night in their season, [21] then My covenant may also be broken with David My servant, so that he shall not have a son to reign on his throne, <u>and with the Levites, the priests, My ministers.</u> [22] As the host of heaven cannot be numbered, nor the sand of the sea measured, so will I multiply the descendants of David My servant and the Levites who minister to Me.'

Christians seem to be familiar with this promise to David, but have (as a whole) failed to also see that the Levites' role is planted right in the middle of David's promise! When God restores the throne of David (worship and kingdom, leadership and authority) and takes up His rightful throne, He is at the same time in the last days restoring the Levites to their role of priests in the kingdom!

According to Rabbi Moshe Joseph Koniuchowsky, the Levites are being restored as "watchmen and prophetic teachers over both houses"[83(para 6)] meaning scattered 10-Israel and Judah. They are to "guard Yahweh's Renewed Covenant Dwelling Place"[83] and "rebuke the devourer (who) sow(s) discord and division." That is a whole lot more responsibility for the Levites than just animal sacrifice.

> We see Levi's latter-day role in Jer(emiah) 33:21-22, being directly tied in by context to verse 24, where Yahweh is said to restore the two chosen families or the two chosen houses of Israel, who will be attended to by the increase in the seed of latter-day Levites. If we understand these fascinating scriptures correctly, we may ascertain that a large portion or even most of Judah or the House of Judah today is composed of Levites, just like most of the nations are composed of Ephramites (10-Israel). Oh the ways and the wisdom of Yahweh! Fill the nations with Ephraim and fill the Judahites with Levi, so that Israel can be all and in all, just as Yahweh Himself is all and in all.[83(para 6)]

SUMMARY OF LEVI

It is especially important to be able to identify Levi in the latter days because as Israel and the Church come together in the end as one new man we will worship together in Jerusalem. Christians have been taught, rightly, that we are all priests and kings before the Lord. However it is the special duty of the Levites to work in the temple. We don't need to argue over whether there will still be sacrifices, because there will still be worship, and the Lord said four times that throughout their generations (perpetually, forever, and never ending) the Levites should receive the tithes and offerings (Numbers 18:8, 11, & 19), and they shall "perform the work of the tabernacle of meeting" (Numb 18:23). If in those days, well-meaning non-Levitical or non-Kohen Christians step up to work in the House of God, they will be getting in the way of the Levites' God-given duties and their inheritance! Selah.

It is imperative not to have your identity so wrapped up in what you do (even do for the Lord) that when things change according to His righteous, good and proper plan, we do not become offended at either our "replacement" or at the Lord. Our identity comes from the Father. Our job in His Kingdom will also come from Him; it won't be second class, but will be perfect for us, because He created both us and our role.

10

THE HOUSE OF JOSEPH:
Ephraim & Manasseh

These two brothers, Ephraim and Manasseh, have been intertwined as tribes and a little different from all the other tribes since the beginning, so we will cover them together too. First, Manasseh and Ephraim were not part of the original 12 sons of Jacob, they were two sons of Joseph, who was Jacob's 11th son. Ephraim and Manasseh were born to Joseph while he ruled in Egypt. They did get to meet their grandpa Jacob though, and they received the birthright blessing from him in place of their father. So in effect, the double blessing that was usually bestowed on the firstborn, not only went to them, but the double blessing was doubled again in that it was bestowed right off to two sons in the next generation. Since Manasseh took Joseph's place, it was Ephraim that became the 13th tribe of Israel, but Jacob switched that order when he placed his right hand on Ephraim and left on Manasseh, leaving Manasseh as number 13 (Genesis 48:17-18). Joseph's sons start out different from the rest of Israel since Manasseh and Ephraim were only half Hebrew because their mother was Egyptian (Genesis 46:20). Early in Israel's history God is demonstrating that He accepts and blesses the Gentile who is joined to the God of Israel.

What comes with the birthright blessing? In the case of the seed of Abraham the birthright entails land, wealth, influence, strength, large population growth, and leadership. (Though *leadership* is not to be confused with the scepter which went to Judah for their role of kingship throughout time.) All of these blessing features were passed to each of the sons, but the birthright is a double portion of those blessings, and that double of everything went to both Manasseh and Ephraim, quadrupling the blessing between them as compared to any other single tribe.

THE GENESIS 48 BLESSING OVER JOSEPH'S SONS

> **Genesis 48:14-16** Then Israel stretched out his right hand and laid *it* on Ephraim's head, who *was* the younger, and his left hand on Manasseh's head, guiding his hands knowingly, for Manasseh *was* the firstborn. [15] And he blessed Joseph, and said: "God, before whom my fathers Abraham and Isaac walked, The God who has fed me all my life long to this day, [16] The Angel who has redeemed me from all evil, Bless the lads; Let my name be named upon them, And the name of my fathers Abraham and Isaac; And let them grow into a multitude in the midst of the earth."

Then is the record of the left-right hand of blessing switching thing for a couple verses, but Jacob knew what he was doing with his right hand on the younger and left hand on the older son.

> **Genesis 48:19-20**[19] But his father refused and said, "I know, my son, I know. He also shall become a people, and he also shall be great; but truly his younger brother shall be greater than he, and his descendants shall become a multitude of nations."

> [20] So he blessed them that day, saying, "By you Israel will bless, saying, 'May God make you as Ephraim and as Manasseh!'" And thus he set Ephraim before Manasseh.
> [21] Then Israel said to Joseph, "Behold, I am dying, but God will be with you and bring you back to the land of your fathers. [22] <u>Moreover I have given to you one portion above your brothers</u> (the birthright portion), which I took from the hand of the Amorite with my sword and my bow." (parentheses added)

The blessing starts with the names of Jacob/Israel, Isaac and Abraham being upon these two sons of Joseph. Then the *"multitude in the midst of the earth"* refers to the population size of these tribes in the latter days. The right hand designated a greater blessing than the left, so Joseph tried to switch Jacob's hands so that his right hand was on the older boy, as was custom, but Jacob was right-hand blessing the younger son on purpose (v.19). Jacob then prophesied that Ephraim would be a *great people*, but that Manasseh would become a *multitude of nations* (v.19). The next blessing is one that holds up Ephraim and Manasseh as the standard of blessing others in Israel (v.20). The last blessing is the double portion above the brothers (v.21), and the last clause alludes to military might (sword and bow) which will be on these brothers in the last days.

In Genesis 49 Joseph is included in the blessing of the Jacob's sons. His blessings also go to his children, Ephraim and Manasseh.

> **Genesis 49:22-26** "Joseph *is* a fruitful bough, A fruitful bough by a well; His branches run over the wall. [23] The archers have bitterly grieved him, Shot *at him* and hated him. [24] But his bow remained in strength, And the arms of his hands were made strong By the hands of the Mighty *God* of Jacob (From there *is* the Shepherd, the Stone of Israel), [25] By the God of your father who will help you, And by the Almighty who will bless you *With* blessings of heaven above, Blessings of the deep that lies beneath, Blessings of the breasts and of the womb.

> ²⁶ The blessings of your father Have excelled the blessings of my ancestors, Up to the utmost bound of the everlasting hills. They shall be on the head of Joseph, And on the crown of the head of him who was separate from his brothers.

There is so much in this prophetic description of Ephraim and Manasseh in the latter days. The House of Joseph will be fruitful (v.22), in a location with plenty of water (v.22), the branches of Joseph will overrun or burst through their boundaries and produce fruit in other nations (v.22). He will be under military attack by people who hate and provoke him (v.23), yet he will remain strong by God's design (v.24). His blessings will come from the heavens and from the deep beneath (underground perhaps) (v.25). He will walk in blessings of high population and health (v.25, breasts and womb). He will surpass the blessings lived by Abraham, Isaac and Jacob (v.26).

> The reason why, in the latter days Joseph is chief among his brethren is, they are closest to God, and because of the (H)oly (S)pirit, God revealed many truths to them. Opened up their minds to the (B)ible, and they ran their nations, and empire by the biblical laws as revealed in scripture. This is why they are fruitful... Ephraim, after it would receive its inheritance of a "company of nations" would send forth its system of (g)overnment, religion, economy, civilization to others so they can be fruitful as well.[56(para 6 "Gen 49")]

MOSES' BLESSING ON THE HOUSE OF JOSEPH

The blessing of Joseph (Ephraim and Manasseh) in Deuteronomy 33 is virtually the same as Jacob's. However, Moses adds the following to Jacob's original blessing:

> **Deuteronomy 33:17** His glory *is like* a firstborn bull, And his horns *like* the horns of the wild ox; Together with them He shall push the peoples To the ends of the earth; They *are* the ten thousands of Ephraim, And they *are* the thousands of Manasseh."

It is common symbols that are found here: the ox is strength and power; the horns are strength, glory and sovereignty as found elsewhere in scrpture.[56] It is quite obvious that Ephraim's empire will be 10 times larger than Manasseh's. The word *push* here can be interpreted as *govern*.[56] "He shall govern the people to the ends of the earth." What nation has ever governed from one end of the earth to the other at the same time besides the British Empire? None. Remember the phrase, "The sun never sets on the British Empire."? We will trace the British royal family line back to David and the House of Judah[29] in the next chapter on Judah, but can the people of the British Commonwealth be traced back to Ephraim through history?

EARLY SIGNS OF DOUBLE BLESSING

POPULATION. In the 40 years between the censuses when coming out of Egypt, the population of Manasseh rose by 20,500 men of fighting age while under difficult circumstances of being mobile in the desert. They went from 32,200 to 52,700 (Numbers 1:35 & 26:34). It was nearly 100% more than the next tribe in line for the number of increase (Asher went from 41,000 to 53,000 people in the same 40 years).

We might expect to see the same rate of population growth among Ephraim, but we don't. They actually decline by 8,000 men. This is probably attributable to the wilderness-era walk-out led by Simeon that we covered earlier (pp. 56-61). However, together the House of Joseph, even with losses among Ephraim, was a "great people" before entering the Promised Land.

LAND INHERITANCE. Manasseh literally received a double portion of land in the inheritance allotments. They divided into half tribes of Manasseh and settled one on each side of the Jordan River (See Map of Inheritance p.28) accounting for twice as much land, and then some, as any other tribe. Ephraim was located just south of West ½ Manasseh in a normal sized portion.

LEADERSHIP. Ephraim was one of the four leader tribes (Reuben, Dan, Ephraim, and Judah) of Israel when they first received instructions on how they were to camp around the Ark of the Covenant in the desert. They used a symbol of an ox or bull, like Judah's was a lion. (This tribal symbol came from the prophecy though, not the other way around).

When entering the Promised Land, the Ark was set up for 400 years as a place of worship in the city of Shiloh, an Ephraimite city.

After Solomon died, and Israel divided into two, the northern kingdom was led by Ephraim, to the extent that the Bible even refers to them as Ephraim (2 Chronicles 25, Hosea). This is the leadership anointing and blessing on Ephraim displayed.

The first king of 10-Israel was Jeroboam, an Ephraimite (I Kings 11:26).

ASSYRIAN EXILE
We have talked several times about 10-Israel being deported by Assyria in waves and some families immigrating to northern lands before they could be taken captive. Those immigrants who came on the scene of history in the 700's BC as the Scythians were called by the name of Isaac. Among those in the north, the "tribe of Manasseh came to be one of the dominant tribes of the Scythians, and the Greeks called them the Massagetae."[55] (Massagatae=Manasseh + an early form of the word Goths).[57] Among those who went with the exile, 10-Israel as a whole became known in Assyria as "Bit Humri" or "khumeri" taken from the name of King Omri of Israel.

> **SCYTHIANS TO SAKA**
> A couple hundred years after they had been living in the Black Sea region and beyond, the Scythians became known as *Saka* or *Sacae* (plural) in Latin once the most ancient forms of Latin were being formed and used by the Romans as they broke away from Greece.

CIMMERIANS. The Assyrians were taken over by the Babylonians and then the Persians, and it was during this time of upheaval that the 10-Israel tribes broke off from the established state and moved westward as the Cimmerians. The Cimmerians were related to the Scythians (since they were all of the House of Israel) but later became known as the Celts as this group continued to migrate over time westward.

PARTHIANS. Another group who were throwing off their Persian masters were the Parthians. Since the P and B sounds are often interchanged in Greek (where we get our historical names) they could also have been from Barthia or Brithia.[55] Remember the connection between BRTH or BRT and the Hebrew word for covenant? It is again written in their name that they were followers of the Covenant. The major branches of the Parthians were the Bactrites, Eranites and Tahanites, which also happen to be the names of three Ephraimite clans named from the sons of Ephraim (Numbers 26:35). Davidiy says, "History records a very close relationship between the Scythians and the Parthians."[49(p.212)] It is reasonable to believe that the Scythians were Manasseh and the Parthians were Ephraim.[55]

> A group of Amyrgian Scythians in the time of Darius, king of Persia, were reported as then dwelling on the Tigris [River] banks. They were led by a chief Saku'ka and revolted against the Persian rulers. In a bilingual inscription these Amyrgians are called Saka Humuvashka in Persian and Gimirri Umurgah in Babylonian. Gimirri [in the Babylonian version] means either 'Tribes' or Cimmerians or perhaps both since the Scyths and Cimmerians were originally one entity.[49(p.360)]

When the Roman Empire began its slow rise to power they were much all about keeping a written record of conquered peoples, their movements and name changes, but they were doing it in a new language that we now call "Old Latin." Besides the difficulty of translating names into a new language, the Romans weren't always accurate in their details.

For example, The Roman record refers to most of the Persian/Scythian tribes using the general term "Germanii" which was the name of only one tribe in Scythia.[57] So during the mid-first century, as the Romans recorded the previous several hundred years history and current happenings, they loosely applied the name of one singular tribe living in the area of Persia to all of the tribes living in that area, and as so it was.[58] They all became known as Germanii or Germans.

SAXONS. There was another "Germanic" tribe of former Scythians or Sakae that the Romans called the "Saxons." Phonetically, "Saxons" is the same as "Sac's sons," or "Sons of Isaac."[57(p.31)] Ptolemy also mentions the Scythian tribes using the name "Saxones."[56] The two are phonetic equals and refer to the same entity.

BECOMING THE ANGLO-SAXONS

One of the major branches of the Parthians who lived in the region of Bactria were called the Bactrites (after one of Ephriam's sons). There was a large sub-tribe living on the edge of Bactria called *Ayghel* or *Aegles*.[56] In Hebrew *ayghel* means bullock (Strong's #5697). These people were most likely of the tribe of Ephraim. Remember that Ephraim was represented by the symbol of a bull which came from the prophetic word given over him and over Joseph from the days when Israel was whole; sub-tribal names came into use to identify people and regions. The Parthians' sub-tribal name distinguishing the Ephraimites (*Aeglah*) when joined with the Saxe or Saxon became known as the Anglo-Saxons.[56]

In the 300's AD the Parthian Empire began to collapse, which is what prodded 10-Israel into joining with their brothers to the north. While Greco-Roman history does record the Parthian collapse, 20th- and 21st-century historians don't seem to make the connections to "the Saxons, Goths and related (so-called) Germanic tribes 'suddenly appearing' in vast numbers as they migrated in search of new homelands, entering Europe from the regions of South Russia and the Black Sea,"[57] which is the exact location of the Parthian collapse. These Saxons and Goths made their way across Europe en masse toward areas where a trickle of their ancestors with a pioneering spirit had set out and settled during the Phoenician Empire period of David and Solomon.

The Romans had conquered Britain, but left around 410 AD with this influx of Scyth, Angle (Aegleh), Saxon and Jute migration.[57] Collins suggests that "Jutes may simply be a variation of the name, Judah or Jats.[57]

THE GOTHS [57]

So the Massagetae retained the name Getae. These were a "a nation of nomads who knew themselves as Gets, Gats, Guts, or Yuts?...[and] the similarity between the Goths, Getae, and the Yuezhi" (article "The Getes" by Sundeep S. Jhutti) is undeniable. [56](as quoted para 1 "The Angles, Jutes and Saxons settle in Britain")

The Goths were of a common origin with the Messagatae, the leading tribe of the Sacae. There is an interesting connection with their name. The background of the word *Goth* in Gothic is *Guth*. *Guth* meant God. English and German languages still use this or a derivative of it to describe the concept of a supreme being today: *God* and *Gott*. The origination of Messagatae's use of Goth in their name could, according to J.C. Gawler, an official of the British government in the 19th century, come from the "kingdom of Arsareth, (who) took the name of Gauthei' because, he says, they were very jealous of the glory of God."[57(para37)] It lends credence to the idea that the Goths did indeed name themselves after God out of their zeal for Him. The Goths emigrated from the same region in Asia where the term "Gauthei" originated. This is logical, not problematic, once it is acknowledged that the Goths or "People of God" are actually the descendants of 10-Israel.

Keep in mind also that many of these people probably had heard the Gospel from the apostles and Rabbi Shaul (Paul) who were on missionary journeys into Asia, and they had been living as Christians for the previous three centuries. We know in particular that the Parthians were well acquainted with the Torah, Tenach, and prophecies of the Messiah. Some of their wise men recognized the signs in the heavens and went to find the Messiah when the star appeared.[69; Matthew 2:2]

Collins synthesizes an *Encyclopedia Britannica* article about the Scythians as they made their way into Europe:

> The *Encyclopedia Britannica* notes that the Greek writers Herodotus and Hippocrates regarded the Sarmatae, or Sarmatians, as a Scythian tribe…(Britannica) confirm(s) that the Scythians were not "lost" in history, but simply became known as "Germans" when they migrated into Europe. We also have seen that many Sacae Scythians came to be known as "Saxons" when they entered Europe, and the Saxons are viewed as a branch of the Germanic tribes. Since many Israelite tribes were known as "Scythians" in Asia, this confirms that many of them were called "Germans" or "Saxons" as they entered Europe.[59]

תא

Ephraim is the Commonwealth of Great Britain

The modern nation(s) associated with the House of Joseph should follow the prophetic statements of Genesis 49 and Deuteronomy 33. The modern British Commonwealth does just that. Even its name, Great Britain, proclaims a fulfillment of prophecy that the Ephraim would be "great" in the latter days! No other nation has ever called itself by the name "great."[66]

"Vined" Out

Great Britain "vined" out like a grapevine, having one central source of grounding (England) but has produced fruit (nations) all over the world beyond the boundaries of her islands. Britain is not just a nation like other nations, but a commonwealth of nations bound together under rule with commonalities among them. While much more extensive in the 1700's-1900's, the Commonwealth nations include the United Kingdom (four nations) plus Canada, Australia and New Zealand. Until 1776, the United States was also included. Great Britain's previous holdings included the United States, South Africa, Hong Kong among many, many others, proving that Ephraim was indeed a "multitude of nations." At one point the British ruled about 1/3 of the world's population and many nations in existence today owe their existence to the British.[66] In 1776, the U.S. broke away from the British Empire becoming the "single great nation that came out of that multitude of nations" (Genesis 48:19).

NATIONS OF "A WELL" OF WATER

Each of the many nations associated with the House of Joseph listed above, both in the past and currently, is not only plentiful in freshwater sources, but is surrounded on three sides by water or are island nations surrounded by water.

MADE STRONG BY GOD IN THE LATTER DAYS

In conjunction to the water statements of fulfillment above, the British also fulfilled this statement of strength by dominating the sea with their navy in the 18th and 19th centuries. As the British Empire began its decline, the U.S. Navy, also of the House of Joseph, fulfilled this role and is currently "the most powerful fleet on earth."[55(para 6)] The alliance of Great Britain, Canada, the U.S., Australia and New Zealand "currently constitute(s) the most cohesive and powerful alliance on earth. God has certainly strengthened the House of Joseph"[61(para 9)] in the latter days, just as He promised!

HATED AND SHOT AT[55]

The nations of Great Britain and the United States have attracted so much hatred and envy in the word that it has commonly been called an "anti-Anglo" or "anti-American" attitude. Much of this hatred has resulted from the envy of other nations who covet the "birthright" promises of the Abrahamic Covenant which were given primarily to the tribes of Joseph (Genesis 48:14-22).[55] Although I am sure they would be loath to know that is what they are jealous of.

Great Britain and the U.S. have been allies fighting together against nations and people who started wars with them, especially in the last 100 years: WWI, WWII, Korean War, Persian Gulf War, and the War on Terror. The instigating nations we have been at war with have been those prophesied "archers" who "hate" and "shoot at" the House of Joseph.

Wealth and Power

The prophecy over the House of Joseph describes "blessings of heaven" which can be interpreted as "favorable climates for growing crops…extensive natural resources (the "blessings of the deep") and large populations ("blessings of the breasts and of the womb")."[61] Blessings of the deep can refer to deep mineral or natural resources from the ground or from the oceans and shores, including the way in which first the British and now the U.S. controls most of the waterways and "world maritime trade."[61]

The nations of the House of Joseph are the richest on earth and some of the largest and most wide spread over the globe.

EVIDENCE IN THE BRITISH COAT OF ARMS

The great seal of Britain, their Coat of Arms, is a shield with a lion guarding one side and a unicorn on the other. The unicorn is synonymous with the wild ox as found in the KJV of Numbers 24:8-9. The lion represents the tribe of Judah who rules the British Commonwealth, the unicorn or ox represents Ephraim who makes up the body of the British people. A depiction of David's harp appears in the bottom left quadrant of the shield.

Photo 1: The British Coat of Arms *in situ*. (c) June 2014 by Greta Zefo

There are two phrases present on the seal: One in Old French which is translated "evil to him who thinks evil" (the "thinking evil *about Britain*" is implied). Doesn't that sound just like God's promise to Israel in Genesis 27:29, "Cursed be everyone who curses you."? The second phrase on the Coat of Arms is "God and my (Birth)right."

Interesting, isn't it? Ephraim, the leading tribe of Israel, son of Joseph used the bull as their symbol. They have carried the birthright blessing through the ages. Jeremiah 31:9 records God declaring, "Ephraim is my firstborn." It is proper for Britain then to declare on their Coat of Arms as a motto of their nation, God and my (birth)right.[56]

"Gatekeepers Blessing" on Abraham and Sarah's Descendants

Another prophecy that gets bypassed sometimes (because there are so many that are fulfilled in the modern nations) is Genesis 22:17, and it is repeated in Genesis 24:60 which both say "Your seed shall posses the gates of their enemies." This promise is again fulfilled in the British and U.S. control of the seas, important ports and waterways. Even physically, when looking at a map, the British Isles lie "like a dominating lion offshore Europe; secure behind the famous English channel, yet guarding the gateway to Europe."[56] The location of Great Britain has been decisive to the outcome of both world wars. But they guard not just the gateway to the Mediterranean Sea. The following statement by Peter Salemi in his article "Ephraim is England and Her Commonwealth" is why "the sun never set on the British Empire" and Great Britain possessed the gates of her enemies:

> During the last of the nineteenth century and much of the twentieth, Britain controlled Palestine, Trans-Jordan, Gibraltar, Malta, Crete, the Suez Canal, The Khyber Pass, the Andaman and Nicobar Islands, Ceylon, Rhodesia, Kenya, and Tanganyika; Singapore and the Straits of Malacca; Hong Kong, Brunei, the Gilberts and Solomons, New Georgia and New Guinea; Santa Cruz. In the Atlantic, Britain controlled the Hebrides, the Falklands, Bermuda, Bahamas, Barbuda, Antigua, St. Vincent, St. Lucia, Barbados, the Cayman Islands, and British Honduras, as well as British Guiana, Gibraltar and Suez, thereby bottling up the Mediterranean, and with Malta, Crete and Cyprus available as naval bases, not to mention Alexandria, in Egypt, as well as the Bosporus Dardanelles between European Turkey and the Anatolian Peninsula, bottling up the Black Sea.
>
> Britain stood astride the most vital sea lanes in the world. Add to this the huge naval base at Singapore and the Straits of Malacca, Hong Kong on the Chinese littoral, together with Brunei. [56]

The British controlled every significant gateway in the world! Could it be any more clear that the hand of God is on this nation as they fulfill the prophecies God spoke to describe Ephraim describing the latter days?

BRITISH FLAG: THE "UNION JACK"[60]

The British flag is called the Union Jack. It comes from the abbreviation of the name James or Jacques to "Jack," or "Jac" as King James VI of Scotland/James I of England signed his name.[60] This name *Jacques* is derived from the ancient Hebrew patriarch Jacob from whom the kings of the British Isles are descended.

> The flag, known as the Union Jack, formed in Great Britain, of the Jacks representing a strong concentration of these peoples has been described, most appropriately, as representing a *"Union of Jacob"*, and thus it has become a point of attack by some who would deny the identification of ourselves with ancient Israel.[60(para 3)]

The stripes come from the Crusader Era during which different colored crosses sewn onto the front of the soldiers' clothing identified people with their nation of origin. The British at first wore white crosses then changed to the red crosses of Saint George. The combination of which forms the red and white crosses on the field of blue found in today's British Standard, the Union Jack.

THE FALL OF THE BRITISH EMPIRE

As it was in the days of Ancient Israel so it is in the modern world. When 10-Israel forsakes worshipping the one true God, He removes His hand of blessing from them for a time to get their attention.

"The British today have forsaken their Christian heritage. Since this dramatic turn from God into materialism, secularism and the like, Great

Britain has been steadily losing her greatness. Many of its overseas protectorates, sea and land gates, and colonies have gone independent."[56] (p.34) God says,

> **Isaiah 28:1-4** Woe to the crown of pride, to the drunkards of Ephraim, Whose glorious beauty *is* a fading flower… To those who are overcome with wine! [2] Behold, the Lord has a mighty and strong one, Like a tempest of hail and a destroying storm, Like a flood of mighty waters overflowing, Who will bring *them* down to the earth with *His* hand. [3] The crown of pride, the drunkards of Ephraim, Will be trampled underfoot; [4] And the glorious beauty is a fading flower.

Dr. Moses Margoliouth says, "all English-speaking peoples of British origin…have played a unique role in history over and beyond that of the other Israelite nations as a whole. This historical record was appropriate to the character of their forefather, JOSEPH."[62(p. 387)] He also says that Israel as a whole was uniquely trained by God in the desert to be a migratory people, Israel was "trained to be a **wandering** nation" with "a peculiar migratory disposition."[62(p.13)]

NEW BRITISH PRINCE GEORGE BAPTIZED WITH JORDAN RIVER WATER! As all things come together in perfect timing to reveal hidden connections, Renee Ghert-Zand's October 24, 2013 headline in *The Times of Israel* reads "Three month-old Prince George is baptized by the half-Jewish Archbishop of Canterbury with water from the Land of Israel"[36] Look at all those connections: The newest member of the British royal family (House of Judah), being baptized by a Jew in water from Israel's Jordan River. Jewish blood in the Royal family is not as unheard of in Britain as it is in the U.S. It is fairly common knowledge, but is not well-acknowledged as to what it might mean. It is the kingly line of Judah ruling over the house of Ephraim who leads her commonwealth around the world (Canada, Australia and New Zealand). And God knew it all from the beginning!

תא

THE UNITED STATES DISPLAYS MANASSEH ORIGINS

With all the complied evidence and general knowledge that Great Britain is the "lost" tribe of Ephraim, how does the United States of America as Manasseh shake out of the rug of history? Many of the above evidences also hold true for a description of Manasseh, of the House of Joseph, too. These two brothers stick together through history and, even currently separated by the Atlantic Ocean, these two nations are closer allies than their common language should provide. The U.S. is a nation of wealth with underground resources such as oil, coal and other minerals, and plenty of fresh water lakes and rivers, some of the largest in the world, in fact. The U.S. has been blessed with its good soil for growing. The breadbasket of America feeds the nations. (Just like Joseph did all those millennia ago!) The U.S. Navy controls the highways of the sea and many ports and waterways.

WHERE DID WE IMMIGRATE FROM?

The United States is generally referred to as a "nation of immigrants." Would it surprise you to know that immigration to the U.S. is not as random as we might have thought?

BACK TO THE ANGLO-SAXON'S INVASION OF BRITAIN.

According to Salemi's research with the Venerable Bede, the Jutes settled in Kent, the Isle of Wight, and parts of Hampshire.[90] The Angles, who are Ephraim, moved and settled in areas of the north and east coast of Britain, including

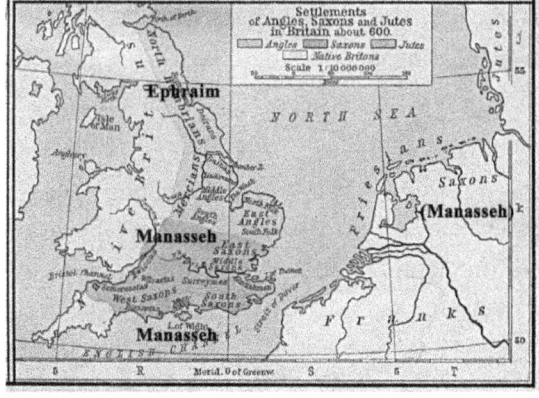

Ephraimite clans of Bercher, Shuetelah and Eran who all settled Northumberland, East, South, and Middle Anglia.[90] "The Saxons that settled in the middle and the south are the Amyrgian Scyths (Sacae) mentioned by Herodotus."[90(para 4 The Angles, Jutes and Saxons settle in Britain)]

Manasseh settled in the south of the island in the kingdom of East Anglia in areas now called
> Norfolk, Suffolk, Cambridge, and part of Lincolnshire. The other Angles (The tribe of Ephraim), who were much more numerous (Deut. 33:17), acquired all the east coast from above modem Edinburgh right down to the present Lincolnshire, as well as the whole of the midlands of England.. The Saxons formed the three kingdoms of Essex, Sussex and Wessex, all in the south of the country. Collectively these tribes were known as the Heptarchy, (i.e. - The land of the Seven Kingdoms)."(Des Thomas, *Iceland Light to the Nations*, p.87).[90(para 6 Angles, Jutes and Saxons)]

More than 80% of the first British settlers in the U.S. came from the specific areas in the British Isles where those who descended from the clans of Manasseh lived together as groups.[63] It was these people, above all others, who formed the U.S. national characteristics.[63]

When Manasseh joined Ephraim in the British Isles, some clans stayed behind in their former homes on the continent, specifically in places such as modern day Germany and Holland.[63] When the U.S. was forming, great contingents of people seeking religious freedom also moved to the New World from the continent. Incidentally the people who came were not just random people fed up with religion-as-usual. They originated in places within those countries or kingdoms associated with the descendants of the tribe of Manasseh. So which counties in Great Britain did they come from? The "Puritans who came, primarily, (were) from East Anglia (and they moved) to the Massachusetts Bay Colony between 1629 and 1640."[90(sidebar)] There were about 80,000 of them who fled England and 21,000 of those settled in the Massachusetts Bay Colony.

"They came from all over England, but most heavily (60%) from the East England counties of Norfolk, Suffolk, Essex, Herfordshire, Cambridgeshire, Huntingdonshire, Lincolnshire, and Kent."[56(sidebar)] When they came though, it is interesting to note that they didn't travel by clan, they made the decision to pick up and move to a foreign, wild place as families.[65] They felt directed by God, and that's because they were! But not necessarily for the reasons they thought. God was moving the bulk of the tribe of Manasseh through individual decisions to the place where He said they would live in the latter days.

The next largest percentage of people immigrating to the U.S. were from the southern counties of England: Dorset, Wiltshire, Devonshire and Hampshire.[90] Accounting for some 10% were cavaliers and servants from the City of London between 1642 and 1675 who came from south Britain to Virginia. For the 50 years, between 1675 and 1725, a group known as the Quakers made their way to Pennsylvania from, predominately, the English midlands.[90] Between 1717 and 1775, the Scotch-Irish made their way to the New World and settled in Pennsylvania and Virginia. They were mostly from "the English/Scottish border counties (sometimes via northern Ireland)"[90]

All of these places mentioned are where the Mercian Saxons settled. Salemi asks if it is "a co-incidence that the United States of America was colonized by mainly the Mercian Saxons, Jutes and Saxons that we can trace back to the tribe of Manasseh?"[90(sidebar)] I think not. It is the plan of God to bring about His promises, His Word and His purposes in the last days!

GERMAN ANCESTRY

In the 2000 censes, 42.8 million U.S. citizens of 273 million claimed German ancestry.[91] That's about one in every six people. Where did most of those folks originate?

K. J. Frolander

Over the decades of the 1800's emigration from Germany varied greatly, influenced by wars in which they were involved. In the 80 years between 1820 and 1900 over 4.5 million Germans sailed for the U.S.[56(sidebar)] As *Encyclopedia Britannica* found, most of them were from the "agricultural areas of northern Germany—West Prussia, Posen, Pomerania, Mecklenburg, Schleswig-Holstein and Hanover, and sometimes the emigration reached 1% of the total population of these provinces."[11th ed., vol. 11) 56 sidebar]

Why are these German provinces special? In 1899, William Ripley published *Races of Europe: A Sociological Study* in which he describes three distinct races found in European nations. "Northwestern Germany—Hanover, Schleswig-Holstein, Westphalia—is distinctly allied to the physical type of the Swedes, Norwegians, and Danes."[68(p. 214)] Most people know there are differences between the northern "low Germans" and the southern "high Germans," but there were also distinctions among the low Germans.[56] Yair Davidiy says,

> In the case of Germany at least would seem to indicate that those [immigrants] who went to the U.S.A. in the 1800s were somehow different from those who stayed behind and German officials themselves remarked on such a difference. The claim for such a distinction is based on consideration of physical types, areas-of-origin within Germany, religious orientation and social outlook.[49(p.430)]

Davidiy traces those Germans to the Heleucones Federation of West Manasseh! Also known as Calucones.[49(p.372)] The immigrants of the first half of the 80-year immigration were mostly farmers establishing farms in the Midwest U.S., from Ohio to the Plains States where even today many in rural areas still claim German heritage. Few Germans settled in the Deep South.[56]

We also have a large contingent of immigrants in the U.S. of Dutch, French and Scandinavian descent. How do they fit into the U.S. being the tribe of Manasseh? They are the descendants of the "remnants of Manasseh when they dwelt in these lands before invading England. French: The 'Sicambian Franks' of France were 'partly of Shechem' (one) clan of Manasseh."[49(p.372)] Among the Dutch of Holland remained the "tribe of Ubii" which are part of Manasseh."[49(p.309)] From Scandinavia (Swedish, Norwegian, Danish) we have the clans of Phiressi, Hearthro, Raumar, and the Hilleviones, which can all be traced to Manasseh.[49(p.373)]

> It is interesting to note that U.S. immigration laws and policies—during much of America's critical, formative years and up until the middle of the 20th century—deliberately favored the peoples of Northwest Europe while, at the same time, limiting white peoples from southern or eastern Europe.[90]

It was the people of the west ½ tribe of Manasseh who made up this second wave of immigration from the German-speaking areas of continental Europe beginning about 20 years after the founding of America. They settled further west in the U.S., in farmland where they could work agriculturally as they were used to. (Notice, they again end up located west of the other half of their tribe, the same way they were originally settled by God in the Promised Land). Most of today's remaining ties to the German language can be found in the Ohio, Pennsylvania, Illinois, Michigan and Florida regions.[67] I also noticed an anomaly in the census data of a strange contingent of German speakers in California;[67] perhaps they are the agricultural owners/operators of the huge food-producing centers there as well.

> Like in the Promised Land, half of Manasseh mainly Machir, Yair and Gilead dwelt in the East, and the rest in the west. The situation in the United States is the same, divided east and west with Machir, Yair, and Gilead in the East, and the rest in the west.[90(para7 Original 13 Colonies)]

It is interesting to note also that it was the Protestant Reformation—a fresh revelation of how we are to relate to God—which brought on all this "moving of the chess pieces" of the world's population into their current, and prophesied, positions.

Manasseh's Name Meaning

There are two meanings of Manasseh. One is "Forgetting" and it is easily found, but there is a hidden meaning found in the connotations in Hebrew. Oddly enough Manasseh means "responsible representation."[63, 66] These two meanings actually work together to describe the United States. Forgetting is a representation of the pioneering spirit that was so prevalent in the first several centuries of Americans.[66] It reminds me of

> **Philippians 3:13b** *Forgetting* those things which are behind and reaching forward to those things which are ahead (emphasis added).

The American pioneer picked up to go west, forgetting all he left behind, whether it be the civilization of the eastern U.S. or the European nation from which he came.

The name *Manasseh* actually foretold our system of government. Manasseh's second meaning of "responsible representation" suggests that "Manasseh would become a Federation of States, yet 'One Nation Under God'."[66(para titled 4)] In Jacob's prophecy he says Manasseh will become a "great people."

> The use of the word *"people"* in contrast to *"company of nations"* is significant, and implies a REPUBLIC, as distinct from a MONARCHY! The term *"people"* is very distinctive, meaning a *"multitude gathered as a unit"*, which is precisely what the United States of America is!
> [66(para titled 4)]

The Naming of America

According to our history books, America was named for Amerigo Vespucci. Finally, something that is correct! But what you may not know is that Amerigo Vespuchi was named "after a Jewish noble named

Americo or Americus"[63] which is the Latin version of the Hebrew name Machir or Ha-Machiri. Which means "belonging to Machir."[63] Manassah's firstborn was a son, named Machir! (Genesis 50:23). Therefore, though it was indirectly, America was named after Machir, Manasseh's oldest son. I think God may have played a role in the naming of this country.

THE U.S. IS OF GREAT STRENGTH & INFLUENCE AFTER BRITAIN IS

This idea of prophetic interpretation comes from the way Jacob crossed his hands as he blessed Joseph's sons. The older son, Ephraim remained on Jacob's right side (strong side) as he should have as the older son, but he received the left hand of blessing (weaker, slower). Manasseh, the younger son, stood on Jacob's left receiving the timing of the spoken blessing second (later in history as well), but received the blessing from Jacob's right hand (his stronger side). Jewish sages agree that this means Ephraim will receive his strength and blessing first and Manasseh to a slower timing, but to a greater degree.

MANY 13'S LINK AMERICA TO ISRAEL'S 13TH TRIBE

There is much ado about the number 13 in relation to the United States. Thirteen original colonies signed the Declaration of Independence to become 13 states. The flag originally contained 13 stripes (and still does today) and 13 stars in a circle. The U.S. motto "E Pluribus Unum" meaning "one of many" or "from many, one" is formed by 13 letters. In taking a look at the great American Seal we find 13 stars in the shape of a "star of David" above the eagle. There are 13 leaves on the olive branch and 13 olives on the branch. There are 13 arrows in the other talon. There are 13 stripes on the shield. The back side of the seal is an unfinished

pyramid with 13 layers under the all-seeing eye of God.

Now all those 13's could just be referring to the original 13 colonies, but perhaps they are referencing a number 13 a little bit further back in our history: when Manasseh became the 13th tribe of Israel.

YANK TO DESCRIBE AMERICANS

The word *Yank* means Jack which comes from an abbreviation of the name Jacob (*Yaacov* in Hebrew). It is what Americans are called all over the world. (Though it is not usually a complimentary term). It is noteworthy, in light of the blessing/prophecy of Jacob that Ephraim and Manasseh will be called after Isaac and Jacob.

A LAST THOUGHT FOR NUMBER CRUNCHERS OUT THERE

Foundation of American States begins in 1787 with Delaware.
American Constitution written in 1787 (ratified in 1789).
Louisiana Purchase in 1803 doubles America's land holdings.

Manasseh was divided into half-tribes of East and West Manasseh in the Land of Israel when they received their inheritance. They also were sent into exile separately, although they followed similar patters of migrations over the millennia. When they were sent out of their inheritance it was prophesied to be for "seven times."

> **Leviticus 26:18** 'And after all this, if you do not obey Me, then I will punish you seven times more for your sins.

What does "times" refer to? In addition to the heaping up of seven portions for one portion in retribution concerning the weight of sin, what if it also referred to the *length* of time? What if God had a specific length of time for 10-Israel's exile when they were removed from the Promised Land, the same way He did for Judah (as told to Jeremiah)? This is a possibility, if we use the Bible to interpret the Bible.

Both Revelation and Ezekiel (Ch 4) refer to a "prophetic" year and day. God describes "time" differently than we Western Greek thinkers (and our calendars!). Revelation 11:2, 11:3 and 12:14 describe the same length of time in several different measurements. "Time, times and half a time" are 42 months, 1,260 days or 3½ years, respectively.

But we are looking for "seven times" not 3½, so we need to double those equal numbers of measurement: 3 ½ years x2= 7 years; 42 months x 2=84 months; and 1,260 days x2= 2,520 days.

And these days/years/months are prophetic in nature, not literal, meaning God wants to say something to His people through them. Like when in the desert, Israel was kept out of the Promised Land one year for every day the spies had been in Canaan and brought back a bad report, so they wandered for 40 years.

> **Numbers 14:34** According to the number of the days in which you spied out the land, forty days, <u>for each day you shall bear your guilt one year</u>, *namely* forty years, and you shall know My rejection.

If we use this same unit of measuring exile punishment and equate it with the sevens mentioned above in the "seven times" of punishment of Leviticus as the payment for sin patterns, it is 2,520 prophetic days or 2,520 years in "ordinary time."[90]

10-Israel's exile came in waves that began in 734 BC with the Assyrians capturing and carrying away two and a half tribes, including East ½ Manasseh.

> **I Chronicles 5:26** So the God of Israel stirred up the spirit of Pul king of Assyria, that is, Tiglath-Pileser king of Assyria. He carried the Reubenites, the Gadites, and the half-tribe of Manasseh into captivity.

The exile continued as 10-Israel fled before capture and bits and pieces were exiled a little at a time until 718 BC when the exile was completed at the end of the three year siege against the capital, Samaria, when the 27,000 people were carried away captive and others were placed in the land by the Assyrians in their place.[7]

An interesting thing shows up when we use the beginning date and the ending date of 10-Israel being sent into exile and add the 2,520 years of promised exile to them. We will also add 1 year because there is no year 0 when switching over from BC to AD.[90]

2,520 (years) – 734 (BC of 1st wave) +1 (yr 0) = 1787 (AD)
2,520 (years) – 718 (BC of last wave) +1 (yr 0) = 1803 (AD)

Significant things occurred in the United States in both of those years!

In the exact part of the world where the two ½ tribes of Manasseh were to be given an inheritance, and would be found in the latter days (as described earlier and prophetically by Jacob and Moses) the Constitution of the United States of America was written in 1787 (it was ratified in 1789). This Constitution was written by a contingent of men from the same counties in Great Britain where the tribe of East Manasseh has been traced across Europe these 2520 years.

In 1803 America made the Louisiana Purchase, doubling their land holdings. The increase in available land in America opened the door for more immigration from European nations such as Germany and Scandinavia. Many of these immigrants were farmers associated in their distant past with West ½ Manasseh. What better land to farm than America's bread basket which feeds the world? According to Salemi, speaking of the Louisiana Purchase,

> That was the greatest acquisition of territory in the history of the United States of America, and West

> Manasseh received their inheritance! Immigration from Germany, Scandinavia, these farmers of Europe immigrated to their birthright homelands, these of West Manasseh![90(p.47)]

Interestingly, Judah's exile of 70 years is also derived from seven times, only using 10 as a multiplier instead. Through the years the people of the Kingdom of Judah had much less struggle with idolatry and other sin issues as compared to the northern Kingdom of Israel's constant struggle. Perhaps that explains the difference in levels of punishment. (But truly, this exile was part of God's plan to prosper His Beloved and the nations).

SUMMARY

Ephraim and Manasseh are the British Commonwealth and the United States, the younger coming out of the older and being greater in the end. They are still joined together in language, culture, power and in our sin issues (which will bring us to downfall if no repentance is to be found, just like in ancient 10-Israel). Even our differences are a bond between us, just as the House of Joseph had in ancient days.

> The birthright name was passed on to Ephraim and Manasseh, "let my name be named on them,..." (Genesis 48:16). Ephraim and Manasseh are rulers over the earth today as God promised. They prevailed over their enemies and become a great nation and a company of nations, and have grown into a multitude in the midst of the earth.[42(para 1 Benjamin)]

God is going about His work to bring about His Word behind the scenes of recorded history, but is revealing identity in this day and age—the latter days—for His purposes and His glory!

11

IDENTIFYING JUDAH

TRIBE OF JUDAH IS THE JEWS

Bet you knew that one! That the Jews are the tribe of Judah is usually uncontested as history; it is fairly easy to follow the people of Judah into a recorded exile that lasted as long as prophesied (70 years) and then a remnant (10%) returned to the very land they had been exiled from, carrying with them the same religious Torah scrolls and language they left with. However it is important to remember that while all Jews are Israelites, not all Israelites are Jews. The names Israel and Judah are not interchangeable in scripture; when God uses a particular name, He is referring to a specific entity and portion of the chosen people.

As we examined with all the other tribes, let's look at prophecy and characteristics of a people to prove modern Jews to be Judah, after all, there was another, much longer exile, and they have returned home again, claiming to be the tribe of Judah, occupying the Promised Land from where they have been scattered over all the earth, having survived multiple attempts of Satan to destroy them throughout their 19 centuries of exile.

Jacob's Prophetic Promise over Judah

> **Genesis 49:8-12** "Judah, you *are he* whom your brothers shall praise; Your hand *shall be* on the neck of your enemies; Your father's children shall bow down before you. ⁹ Judah *is* a lion's whelp; From the prey, my son, you have gone up. He bows down, he lies down as a lion; And as a lion, who shall rouse him? ¹⁰ The scepter shall not depart from Judah, Nor a lawgiver from between his feet, Until Shiloh comes; And to Him *shall be* the obedience of the people.
> ¹¹ Binding his donkey to the vine, And his donkey's colt to the choice vine, He washed his garments in wine, And his clothes in the blood of grapes. ¹² His eyes *are* darker than wine, And his teeth whiter than milk.

Picking out the main descriptions we find that Judah's brothers will praise him, he shall control his enemies, his kinsmen will bow to him. Paradoxically Judah is represented by a lion's whelp (young) and an old lion who hunts prey. The scepter (or kingly leadership) will pass through Judah's bloodline. Then the prophecy starts a description of "Shiloh" who seems to be associated heavily with Judah and attached to these agricultural words like *vine* and *wine*.

Lion's Whelp and Old Lion

Let's start with the paradox. Young and old simultaneously? Yet isn't that exactly what the modern nation of Israel is? They trace their history back 3,000 continuous years, and yet they celebrated their 65th birthday May 15, 2013! A nation "born in a day" (Isaiah 66:8) in 1948! Zephaniah 2 even locates this new-old nation in the land formerly known as Judea just prior to "the day of the Lord."

> **Zephaniah 2:6-7**: The seacoast shall be pastures, With shelters for shepherds and folds for flocks. ⁷ The coast

shall be for the remnant of the house of Judah; They shall feed *their* flocks there; In the houses of Ashkelon they shall lie down at evening. For the LORD their God will intervene for them, And return their captives.

"YOUR HAND SHALL BE ON THE NECK OF YOUR ENEMIES"

This phrase indicates that Judah will be mighty in warfare. When Zephaniah 12:6's prophecy of Judah "devouring her enemies" is added, it looks like Judah will be a devastating force when she is returned to the land which God promised. And in the State of Israel's 65 years, she has been at war about 75% of her days. It is mandatory for citizens to serve military time, and Israel is a mighty military force far beyond the Middle East. Every war has been started by her neighbors (usually ganging up on her 5:1), and almost every war has ended with an Israeli victory and increased land holdings for Israel. The U.S. military teachers at West Point refuse to teach on modern Israeli wars because the outcomes are too miraculous. They cannot be duplicated![85] The Israeli military functions like a bold predator, putting her hands around the throat of her enemies, when necessary.

JUDAH AS AGRICULTURALISTS

When Jews began to immigrate back to Palestine (formerly Judea and Samaria) in the 1800's, the land lay in disastrous ruin: swamps full of malaria-carrying mosquitoes and full-on desert climate everywhere else. In fewer than 150 years Israel has been transformed to a flower in full bloom. The swamps of the north have become virulent farms, not only feeding Israel's burgeoning population, but also exporting to Europe. The deserts of the south have been irrigated and now stands of palm trees produce dates enough to export. In addition, the irrigation technology is being exported to other desert regions of the world so that again in Judah have all nations been blessed. Isaiah prophesied this abundance.

> **Isaiah 35:1** "The wilderness and the wasteland shall be glad for them, And the desert shall rejoice and blossom as the rose."

FATHER'S CHILDREN SHALL BOW BEFORE YOU

In what has been the second most miraculous turn of events in Israel's history (the nations returning is most miraculous), in the last 40-50 years the Christians in the nations have gone from hating the Jews (and some even supporting the Nazi "solution" in Europe for getting rid of the Jews) to the majority of Evangelical Christians embracing the returning Jews as "the chosen people." Christians in the nations are by far the biggest supporters of the Jewish people politically, emotionally and financially as they thrive in a hostile "neighborhood." Christians repenting after perpetrating or not intervening in the Holocaust has gone a long way toward softening the hearts of our Jewish brothers toward us. But what we Christians don't fully grasp yet, is that the Jews—the tribe of Judah—are our brothers in more than just the spiritual aspect of brotherhood. We recognize and honor the Jews of the tribe of Judah as Sons of Abraham because we *have something to recognize them by!* Biblical Law: they keep the Torah and eat according to Levitical law, (or know they should); they celebrate the Feasts of the Lord, and rest on the Sabbath. They identify with their tribe.

We don't recognize ourselves as their tribal brothers because we rejected the law and were cast out (or left) without our Covenant identities in Yahweh. "If the descendants of the ten tribes had also retained these biblical customs throughout history, their Israelite heritage would never have become obscured."[29(para 6)] The ancestors of 10-Israel walked away from God's hand of correction in rebellion, but His hand of blessing did not leave them. Whether they recognize their identity or not, each tribe is functioning according to God's Word, His prophecies concerning the 10 tribes of Israel. And the Christians of the nations of 10-Israel support Judah. Other nations' Christian populations are learning to as well.

IDENTIFYING JUDAH

THE DYNASTY OF DAVIDIC KINGS

Besides the obvious Jesus/Yeshua-Shiloh-David's line-Eternal Kingdom-Kingship connections here, since David and Solomon "there have **always** been Israelites of the various tribes ruled by monarchs descended from David and Solomon." 29(para7) Not just Israelite tribes have been ruled by David's line though, when considering the Scythian and Parthian Empires and their movements into Europe as Cimmerians, Celts and Gauls "the hereditary ruling houses of Europe can be traced to Davidic kings who once ruled over Scythian kingdoms and the widespread Parthian Empire of the ten tribes [in Asia] (which) fulfills the prophecy of Genesis 49:3 and 10."29 (para 7) The kings of England, through the royal house of Ireland and Scotland, can continuously trace their ancestry back to the ancient kings of Judah.29 Reverend A.B. Grimaldi compiled the complete list of the dynasty from Adam to Queen Victoria who was ruling in the 1800's when the list was written, saying, "We have always been able to trace David's seed to Queen Tephi, of Ireland, who was the daughter of Zedekiah..."30(end remarks) Frequent intermarriages among royalty of European nations and the British royalty over the centuries continued to spread a traceable line of King David's seed29 until the House of Judah has touched every nation where 10-Israel is found. Just as God promised, David will never lack a son to sit on Israel's throne!

When Judah was exiled the second time (70 AD), they wandered Europe and the globe as transportation options opened up travel. Yet they kept their identity because they clung to the Covenant and to Yahweh as their God. And the Lord brought them back to the Promised Land, right on time.

LEVITES BACK IN THE PARTHIAN/BARTHIAN EMPIRE

A little Christmas connection. I am pretty sure you already have had "the three wise men" story debunked as some sermon point in your Christmases past, as it was three gifts, not three men. But here is something you may not have been taught: The phrase "from the east" in most of our translations has been translated or shortened to this phrase.

The wise men were actually from "beyond the Euphrates" which is a euphemism for Parthia, where part of 10-Israel was dwelling in the days of Jesus.[80] (This euphemism can be compared to the American phrase "other side of the Rio Grande." You know that I am talking about Mexico with that phrase.)

> **Matthew 2:1-3** Now after Jesus was born in Bethlehem of Judea in the days of Herod the king, behold, wise men from the East came to Jerusalem, ² saying, "Where is He who has been born King of the Jews? For we have seen His star in the East and have come to worship Him."
> ³ When Herod the king heard *this,* he was troubled, and all Jerusalem with him

Have you ever wondered 1. why God would reveal Jesus in the stars to a bunch of random pagans in the east? (which begs the question "why not reveal it to Judah?") and 2. why Herod and all Jerusalem were scared of some wise men in town?

Here is the backstory to the Magi's* arrival in Jerusalem. The Parthians (10-Israel) had been at war with Rome on and off for about 100 years. War was off, in a "shaky peace" at the time of Jesus' birth.[80] Parthia had been living under kings from the royal line of David-in-exile (those who had not returned from the 586 BC or exile or "lost" 10-Israel) for centuries. Second Kings 25:27-28 says that Babylon released Jehoiachin and appointed this last king of Judah to rule over (presumably) his kindred people, 10-Israel whom Babylon had "inherited" when Babylon conquered Assyria.

> **2 Kings 25:28** He spoke kindly to him, and gave him a more prominent seat than those of the kings who *were* with him in Babylon.

---

* *Magi* doesn't necessarily mean "magic" even though it sounds similar in English

Why would Babylon give rulership to a different king-in-exile who didn't understand the people he was supposed to rule? The Parthian line of kings were referred to as Arsacids and their priestly line was called the Megistanes.[80] *Megistane* is a Greek word (Strong's #3175) which means "great men or lords." "It is well known that the Arsacids were descendants of the last king of Judah, Jehoiachin"[80 (para 3 "Levi among Israel")] and therefore in the line of David. The Megistane priests or Magi of Parthia, were Levitical priests who were in exile with Judah and functioned according to God's promise:

> **Jeremiah 33:17-18** "For thus says the LORD: 'David shall never lack a man to sit on the throne of the house of Israel; [18] nor shall the priests, the Levites, lack a man to offer burnt offerings before Me, to kindle grain offerings, and to sacrifice continually.'"

Daniel, a wise young Judahite man, was taken captive to Babylon with Judah in the first wave of the siege of Judea in 605 BC. He became an advisor to at least four recorded kings in scripture, and perhaps as many as 12 kings since there was so much turmoil in his lifetime. Daniel was given this exalted title of Megistane too.[87] As centuries passed, and new empires rose (Babylonian to Medo-Persian to Greek to Roman) the Magi became more and more influential because of their wisdom. It came about that the Magi's wisdom was consulted on the naming of new kings.[87]

In the beginning of the first century AD, Parthia threw off their king "in search of a different kind of king."[80(para 7)] Having followed the sign of a star in the heavens, the Megistanes thundered into Jerusalem with an escort of a 1,000-man mounted cavalry, because according to Parthian history, that's how they always traveled.[87] Back to our two questions.

HOW DID THEY KNOW ABOUT THE STAR? The Parthian Megistanes, or Magi knew about the star because they were the Levitical priests. They grew up studying the prophecies of ancient Israel, and not-so-ancient Israel. They knew the scripture; it is where they got their wisdom. They were anointed as priests throughout their generations in an appointment by God. The Magi of old were also well known as astronomers—(not astrologists!). They studied the stars, and could read what God was saying in the night sky. Long before Satan corrupted astronomy with his backward lie of astrology, the story of Creation and Redemption was written there in the 48 true constellations of the Zodiac for all mankind to read and understand.[88] Here is a link to provide a foundation if you are interested in further study: http://www.asis.com/users/stag/zodiac.html.[88]

The Parthian Magi of Levi knew what to look for, and were actively looking, that is how they saw the star and recognized its significance. God was speaking to these men who were looking for Him.

WHY WAS HEROD UPSET?

Herod was so scared his knees were knocking! *Etarachtha* is the Greek word translated as "troubled" in Matthew 2:3; it actually means 'to shake violently.'[87] Herod was shaking because the Parthian "kingmakers were on his doorstep and they were not looking for him."[87 para 7]

> The Wise Men: It was horses, not camels, and a thousand men, not three. Good luck with that Nativity scene this year!

The Magi's identity as Levitical priests to Judah and Israel in exile is not only how they found the Messiah, but how they recognized that it was not for this time that they should snatch Him up and crown Him king of Parthia.

JUDAH AND ISRAEL WILL REMAIN SEPARATE ENTITIES UNTIL THE FINAL LAST DAYS

Some people have a problem accepting the Jews as Judah because the Jews have not accepted Yeshua as the Messiah as the rest of 10-Israel has, but yes—you guessed it!—there's a prophecy about that!

Zechariah begins the chapter 12 prophecy of the latter days by setting up that the House of Israel and House of Judah are still separate. And the House of Judah is correlated with Jerusalem (and her "cup of trembling" to the nations). Then Zechariah writes prophetically,

> **Zechariah 12:10-11a** And I will pour on the house of David and on the inhabitants of Jerusalem the Spirit of grace and supplication; then they will look on Me whom they pierced. Yes, they will mourn for Him as one mourns for *his* only *son,* and grieve for Him as one grieves for a firstborn. ¹¹ In that day there shall be a great mourning in Jerusalem...

It is only at the very end that Judah will understand that Yeshua, whom they (the tribe of Judah's leadership) pierced, was and is the long-awaited Messiah. I think they will mourn for their blindness, for their lost time, their lost relatives, for their sin.

There are no other peoples on earth who fulfill all these descriptions of the tribe of Judah in these latter days. The Jews are the tribe of Judah.

But Judah and 10-Israel will be reunited in the end, part of the "One New Man" Rabbi Sha'ul (Paul) describes prophetically in Ephesians 2:15. And 12,000 from each tribe will be sealed, 144,000 in total! No one will be lost, because Yahweh knows where He puts each person. In the greatest game of hide-n-seek ever, He is the Great Seeker of those who have hidden themselves from His light and those He has hidden away (even if they didn't know He has hidden and reserved them!) until that Last Great Day when He will reveal, uncover, unite and unveil them as a strong, beautiful Bride for His Son!

12

IMPLICATIONS OF THE LOST TRIBES FOUND

How could these huge numbers of 10-Israel in Western nations be correct?

Well, just three generations ago in the 1930's-40's the combined tribes of Judah and Benjamin with some Levites included, numbered nine million. This population of Jews had been under pressure, persecution and forced removal from their various homes for nearly 2,000 years of exile from their homeland. Several times in Europe, Spain and Russia especially, there were massacres of Judah and forced conversions. And yet, in the 1930's there still were nine million Judahites (with Benjamites) throughout Europe and western Asia. It makes sense that if 10-Israel was given an extra 1,000 years and three times as many tribes on the front end, in addition to living under much less persecution the whole time, and being blessed by the birthright birthrate blessing in the tribes of Ephraim and Manasseh that 10-Israel would be numbering in the millions upon hundreds of millions by now. Just as is shown in this study. Perhaps a better description is that Israel now numbers as the "stars of the sky" or the "sands of the seashore" (Genesis 15:5 & 22:17).

There is another prophecy blessing given by Noah over his sons, Ham, Shem and Japheth, that gives some more understanding to the enlargement of the Hebrews among the nations up to these latter days. Ham is referred to in this section by the name of his son, Canaan.

> **Genesis 9:26-27** And he said: "Blessed *be* the LORD, The God of Shem, And may Canaan be his servant. 27 May God enlarge Japheth, And may he dwell in the tents of Shem; And may Canaan be his servant."

The Hebrews, all tribes, are descended from Shem, as are most of the other Middle Eastern people groups (though not Egypt). The descendants of Japheth [which, incidentally, sounds like the Hebrew word for "enlarge."[(NIV footnote)]] spread east across Asia (Russia, Japan, China, etc.) becoming the most populous of people groups in the world.[86] Just like God said they would. Some of Japheth explored westward with Shem, but not as the Caucasians the way we've been taught. "Caucasians" are people from the Caucasus Mountains region (located between the Black and Caspian Seas) who traveled west into Europe at the exact time as we have established that the tribes of 10-Israel made their way over land into Europe as the former Scythians, Parthians, Cimmerians, Goths, Jutes, Germans, Saxons and Vandals.[86] The Caucasians and 10-Israel are one and the same! The Caucasians are Semitic tribes fulfilling Abraham's prophecy of becoming a great nation (Genesis 12:2) and a company of nations (Genesis 17:4-5). Thomas Lessman[89] has some brilliant maps available on his website for tracing movements century by century, http://www.worldhistorymaps.info/

We don't think of Caucasians as Semites for two reasons. First, "Caucasian" is now used as a more palatable name of the White race or Aryan race. Second, the word *anti-Semitic* has come to mean "anti-Jewish" (as in tribe of Judah) from the time leading up to the Holocaust,[86] because those were the only chosen people who had been revealed at that time. The "Jewishness" that the world hates through the

IMPLICATIONS

word *anti-Semitic*, is the Hebrew tribe who knows his identity, clings to the Laws and Word of God and displays the ancient promise and faithfulness of God Eternal.

Obviously the world tosses the atheistic and secular Jews into the same pile as observant Jews. Satan, working through world opinion, doesn't care if the Jews are observant or not, it is *who* they are that is bothersome to him. And the world is right in this assessment! Because in the End, secular and observant Jews alike will look upon the One whom they pierced and will recognize Him and repent and accept His sacrifice as payment for their sins! (Zachariah 12:10; John 19:34-37)

This asserting that Europe is mostly Shem, not Japheth, brings up another whole balygan of questions. Did 10-Israel perpetrate the Holocaust of their brothers—Judah and Benjamin? Did they just not recognize them as relatives and 10-Israel's hearts were (unknowingly) jealous over the relationship Judah had with God and their identity as God's chosen people, which really was 10-Israel's identity too, but they forgot it (or were purposefully misled by the father of lies)?

Maybe, maybe not. How is that for a precise answer? We know that when Babylon conquered the Assyrians, some Assyrians and most of 10-Israel fled west. As we studied under "Gad," the Assyrians/Prussians were found in East Germany when God brought remnants of Manasseh out of Germany into America. Then the Medes and Persians ruled that same area of Babylon. Then the Seleucids took over. Then the Parthians dominated. Then Rome tried but couldn't conquer the Parthians. The Persians regained power in Babylon as the Parthians went west. In the 700's AD the Muslim Empire began to spread throughout this entire Japheth and Shem area with persecutions and their scimitar of death. People converted, died, or moved on. A culture of death invaded and set up a stronghold in this plot of land called Babylon in the Middle East way back at the time of the Tower of Babel, and this evil has been perpetuated at various intensities throughout time. That same culture of death surrounded Hitler and his upper echelons in Germany, whether Hitler was of the lineage of Shem (and 10-Israel) or Japheth (and the Prussians) doesn't really matter. It was the sickness of death in his heart that invited the devil to carry out his plan to destroy God's chosen people and ultimately work toward making God a liar.

It was the sins of jealousy and pride among Christian nations (most of whom hated the Jews at that time) that opened Satan's entryway for the culture of death that overtook Europe for several decades. Europe's death culture was perpetuated by a lack of identity among those who participated (willingly or not). What lengths would 10-Israel of Europe, Great Britain (and all her colony nations) and America have gone to in order to protect their brothers, the Jews, if only they had known? I think Hitler would have been stopped in his tracks with *Mein Kampf* and never been elected president!

The Holocaust situation sheds new light on this prophetic verse:

> **Hosea 4:6a** My people are destroyed for lack of knowledge

BUT THESE NATIONS AREN'T GODLY NATIONS

Obviously none of these 10-Israel modern nations have done life and government 100% correctly. They were birthed in idol worship and rebellion—fleeing from God's correction in the 700's BC—so how could they? However each of these nations was founded on or maintains a moral code based on the Ten Commandments found in the Torah.

There cannot be a nation completely surrendered to God's kingship and government while any man besides Yeshua sits on the throne. Looking at probabilities, it is likely that people of 10-Israel living in mainland Europe were among those who persecuted their brothers the Jews, in Spain, in Russia, in France, in Germany. And certainly during the Holocaust. That is the kind of horror that develops in a man's heart when living outside of his identity and destiny, apart from the God who made him.

One day Jesus will rule a perfect kingdom from His throne in Jerusalem for 1,000 years! And hopefully that thousand years will *not* seem as though a day!

תא

WHY HIDE THIS HISTORY?

Remember who is out to make God a liar: Satan. He is the one behind these historical cover ups. People who have not yielded control of their lives to God are subject to Satan's influence. Since God has declared time and time again that He is *for* Israel, then anyone who is against Israel is against God, and they are therefore perpetuating the devil's version of history. This subjugation can be as outright as our current generation of Iranian leadership provides by screaming that the Holocaust never happened. Or subjugation to Satan's lies can be as unnoticeable as the pride of a conquering nation renaming an area (like Palestine) to wipe out Israel's history of God keeping His Word to care for and prosper Israel, even during the punishment of exile.

Historian Steven Collins' take on this hidden history of the chosen people is this,

> It is not that historians have been unable to follow their (10-Israel) migrations, but rather, that most have refrained from trying. We have the Scythians, Parthians, Gauthei, and related peoples "suddenly appearing" in Asia with Hebrew names and customs just after the Israelites migrated to Asia.[57]

Collins also says,

> "History texts are full of information about Gentile empires, but omit or downplay the history of the Israelite empires (Phoenicia, Carthage, Parthia, and Scythia), even though the Israelite empires frequently defeated the

> Gentile empires of Assyria, Persia, Greece, and Rome in wars."[29]

Satan has tried again and again to get God to break His Word, His covenant, with the whole of Israel. Satan has tried introducing sin to the earth. He set himself up as idols to receive the worship that belongs to our Creator. He twice tried to murder the saviors God raised up for His chosen people (Moses and Jesus). He set up horrific persecutions to get the Hebrew people to curse God. Satan tried to steal the Promised Land. He arranged a modern extermination of the known chosen people. Satan hates all of God's people, because God loves us. Satan's argument is not even with us; it is all an attempt to usurp God's place. But Satan will never win. God will never fail! Satan's end has already been written by the God who never lies and who never fails to keep His Word.

God says, "I am watching over My Word to perform it" (Jeremiah 1), and he will never forget Israel since He says, "I have engraved you on the palm of my hand" (Isaiah 49:16). The most amazing thing about God's unfolding history story is that the end has already been written, even from the Beginning. It is not unfolding to Him, only to us. He has already decreed that Satan's final act will be burning in the lake of fire (Revelation 19 and 20), and our final act will go on forever. We will live forever as the Bride of the Son of the Living God!

> **Revelation 21:3-4** And I heard a loud voice from heaven saying, "Behold, the tabernacle of God *is* with men, and He will dwell with them, and they shall be His people. God Himself will be with them *and be* their God. [4] And God will wipe away every tear from their eyes; there shall be no more death, nor sorrow, nor crying. There shall be no more pain, for the former things have passed away."

Our faithful Creator will make all things new by His Word!

Conclusion of the Tribes of Israel

Isn't it interesting to note that the nations who in the later days would be called the 10 "lost tribes" are found to have been the Christian nations of the world? In Europe, even from the time of Jesus to the Middle Ages as the gospel of Jesus spread across the world, it was accepted by those of the House of Israel and those who hosted them, while it was rejected by the majority of people in lands who serve other or many gods. Of course Christians are found in every nation of the earth, but everywhere you find Christianity influential to culture and society, there is a nation derived from the people of ancient 10-Israel.

Generations of 10-Israel have made horrible mistakes and have fallen into sin patterns that destroyed their civilizations, and yet, Christianity endured. Though considered to be the "Gentile nations," it is mostly these nations that are full of the ancestors of ancient 10-Israel who have accepted the God of Abraham, Isaac and Jacob and His son, Jesus as their own. China, the Middle Eastern countries, India, Japan, even though they currently influence world politics, are not considered "Christian nations" whereas the U.S., Great Britain, Australia, New Zealand, even France, Spain, the Netherlands and Scandinavia have a foundation of the Bible as their moral guide. In South America too, where a majority of the populous is of Spanish origins, they have a Christian foundation, though they don't have much world influence currently.

Implications

What are the implications of 10-Israel being found all over the world, especially for a Christian that finds out that *you* are 10-Israel? I suppose a whole other book could be written as God continues revealing His story, plans and purposes. But it seems to me that the short of it is that we, with this new-to-us revelation, would need to read the Bible over again as if for the first time, and really look for God's instructions in the Books of the Law (Torah) given to Israel when they (we) were whole. We should read the books of history as *our* historical past, *our* ancestors, who were imperfect people that God used anyway, because He loved them.

We should not be afraid to take our "why's" to God concerning His laws. The veil between us and the Father has been torn, and He was the one who tore it! We were made for relationship, and relationship includes not just blindly following someone, but digging deeply into their hearts to discover the thoughts and intents of their decisions. We can rest assured that God did not just make up random rules to make life difficult, but that there was thoughtfulness and care behind each law.

We should learn from Ancient Israel's sin and mistakes—what good is an object lesson if we ignore the lesson?—and copy the ways in which they walked the straight path of righteousness and bring glory to our Father. We should learn who the Father is and how He related to us in ancient Israel and search the Scriptures for how we can better relate with Him now.

Following Torah

Something that may seem like an implication of Israel being found among modern Christian nations is the age-old question of whether Gentile Christians have to follow Torah. First-generation disciples dealt with this at the Council of Jerusalem as recorded in Acts 15. It seemed good to them and the Holy Spirit to only *require* four things of gentile Christians.
1. abstain from things offered to idols
2. from blood
3. from things strangled
4. from sexual immorality.

This scripture relating the list of four does not say that you *cannot* follow the other aspects of Torah, only that it is not a requirement to stand as one called by Jesus' name. Just like when a Buddhist becomes a Christian it is not mandatory for him to start celebrating Christmas and Easter. It is a privilege. Perhaps in the same way, the Lord "wonders" why we Christians have not held in high regard the Feasts of the Lord described in the foundations of our Scriptures as a time the Lord Himself set aside to meet with all His people.

So why these four restrictions and no more? All four of these commands are related to recognizing who a person is worshipping. Ancient worship practices included offering things and food to idols, blood sacrifices, strangling animals and humans and temple prostitution. The Holy Spirit and the Believing Leaders at the Jerusalem Council wanted to be sure the Jews and the Gentiles knew whom they were worshipping. Beyond forsaking all other gods to worship the God of Abraham, Isaac and Jacob, everything else is window dressings. Remember, the Torah was God's Word given as a Constitution of a new nation as they escaped the slavery of Egypt. Torah is God's instructions to "stay on the path" of righteousness so that Israel would be set apart from other nations for a specific purpose (holy). The Word of God brings about righteousness when followed with a pure heart. Torah was never mandatory; holiness and righteousness cannot be forced. (A more thorough explanation can be found in *Israel II: Beyond the Basics*, chapter 5.)

Disobeying the instructions in the Torah is sin, and sin always leads to destruction. Sin doesn't keep you out of heaven. Not accepting Jesus' payment for your sin is what disqualifies someone from eternity with God. In this Age of Grace (the empowerment to avoid sin) and Mercy (forgiveness after we've sinned) we are instructed by our relationship with the Holy Spirit as our understanding agrees with the Word of God (Old and New Testaments). As the Holy Spirit convicts each individual of the way in which he or she should live, the outflow of that relationship is changed behavior toward purity, righteousness, humility, true justice and more. But instead of the changed behavior being a result of following a list of rules, it is a daily act of worshipping our King. The attitude is the difference!

STANDING WITH ISRAEL

As the nations of Europe, the British Commonwealth, and the Americas, our shared brotherhood with Ancient Israel is another reason to stand with the new Nation of Israel as God is restoring her. We should be viewing the State of Israel not as "them" but as "us." Obviously not as any replacement of the House of Judah, but as co-heirs of the promise of Abraham. Not as a better-than, full-knowledge co-heir, but as an equal partner with a different destiny. Gentile Christians of the nations also have a role in this great kingdom God is forming. No one gets left out and everyone who accepts Yeshua as God's Son and Savior gets to play.

What is your role in the Kingdom and how are you fulfilling it?

END NOTES CHAPTER 1

1. Birch, D. 2005. Iranian president makes pitch to radicals. *The Baltimore Sun.* Retrieved February 26, 2014 from http://articles.baltimoresun.com/keyword/holocaust-denial
2. Avilia, O. April 25, 2007. Lawmakers legalize abortion within Mexico City. *The Chicago Tribune.* Retrieved February 26, 2014 from http://articles.orlandosentinel.com/2007-04-25/news/MMEXABORT25_1_abortion-on-demand-abortion-measure-mexico-city
3. Retrieved February 26, 2014 from http://www.knoxnews.com/news/2012/mar/21/lenoir-city-school-system-curtailing-prayers-at/
4. Gray, R. April 3, 2010. Missing link between man and apes found. *The Telegraph.* Retrieved February 26, 2014 from http://www.telegraph.co.uk/science/evolution/7550033/Missing-link-between-man-and-apes-found.html
5. Jewish Population in Israel statistics http://www.jewishvirtuallibrary.org/jsource/Society_&_Culture/newpop.html
6. Mallowan, Max. 2014. Encyclopaedia Britannica. Nineveh. Retrieved August 19, 2014 from http://www.britannica.com/EBchecked/topic/415684/Nineveh.
7. Rhodes, Melvin. 1995-2014. Seven prophecies that must be fulfilled before Jesus Christ's return. *The Good News.* United Church of God, an International Association. Retrieved August 19, 2014 from http://www.ucg.org/doctrinal-beliefs/seven-prophecies-must-be-fulfilled-jesus-christs-return/

END NOTES CHAPTER 2

1. Klier, John. 2010. YIVO Institute of Jewish Research. Pogrom info retrieved October 13, 2012 from http://www.yivoencyclopedia.org/article.aspx/Pogroms
2. moved Israeli stats info to chapter 1
3. McGrew, Warren. 2013, January 11. Retrieved April 7, 2014 from http://wmcgrew.blogspot.com/2013/01/the-finger-prints-of-god.html
4. http://www.wordoftruthradio.com/questions/48.html
5. Ephraim meaning retrieved October 15, 2013 from http://www.abarim-publications.com/Meaning/Ephraim.html

6. Dan meaning retrieved October 15, 2013 from http://www.abarim-publications.com/Meaning/Dan.html
7. Reuben's name meaning retrieved October 15, 2013 from http://www.abarim-publications.com/Meaning/Reuben.html
8. Gad's name meaning retrieved October 15, 2013 from http://www.abarim-publications.com/Meaning/Gad.html
9. Benjamin's name meaning retrieved October 15, 2013 from http://www.abarim-publications.com/Meaning/Benjamin.html
10. Asher meaning retrieved October 15, 2013 from http://www.abarim-publications.com/Meaning/Asher.html
11. Manasseh meaning retrieved October 15, 2013 from http://www.abarim-publications.com/Meaning/Manasseh.html
12. Simeon's name meaning retrieved October 15, 2013 from http://www.abarim-publications.com/Meaning/Simeon.html
13. The meaning of Issachar "NOBS Study Bible Name List reads Man Of Hire. Jones' Dictionary of Old Testament Proper Names reads He Is Wages. BDB Theological Dictionary favors There Is Recompense." Retrieved October 15, 2013 from http://www.abarim-publications.com/Meaning/Issachar.html
14. Zebulon's name meaning retrieved October 15, 2013 from http://www.abarim-publications.com/Meaning/Zebulun.html
15. small view tribes found retrieved October 15, 2013 from http://www.cohen-levi.org/the_tribe/tribes_of_israel.htm
16. Hooker, Richard. 2013. The Two Kingdoms. Retrieved October 16, 2013 from http://www.jewishvirtuallibrary.org/jsource/History/Kingdoms1.html
17. Map listed under "free maps" from Public Domain Retrieved October 16, 2013 from http://www.biblenews1.com/maps/maps.html
18. Collins, Steven M. 2013. StevenMCollins.com Speeches: Ten Tribes I. Retrieved October 16, 2013 from http://stevenmcollins.com/html/speeches.html.
19. Josephus. *Antiquities of the Jews XI*, Chapter 5, v.2. Retrieved October 17, 2013 from http://www.sacred-texts.com/jud/josephus/ant-11.htm
20. Schmidt, Roderick. 2008. The Equinox Project. *Clifford Baldwin and the Inyo Zodiac*. para 5. Retrieved October 17, 2013 from http://www.equinox-project.com/zodia.htm
21. Ersjdamoo Blog. September 25, 2012. Davenport Stele Is "Rosetta Stone"? Retrieved October 17, 2013 from http://www.equinox-project.com/zodia.htm
22. "America's Stonehenge" retrieved October 17, 2013 from http://en.wikipedia.org/wiki/America_Unearthed

23. Ancientdigger.com. Nov 27, 2009. Retrieved October 17, 2013 from http://www.ancientdigger.com/2009/11/ohio-decalogue-stone-ten-commandment.html
24. Beck, Glenn. (n.d.). Fox News. Minute 3:11 Retrieved October 17, 2013 from the clip found at http://www.youtube.com/watch?feature=player_embedded&v=6oZ1DZd8Xuc
25. Welch background retrieved October 17, 2013 from http://en.wikipedia.org/wiki/Welsh_people
26. The questions of research for finding the 10 tribes originally formulated by Hanok from Jews and Joes.com. 15 June, 2009. Retrieved October 18, 2013 from http://jewsandjoes.com/the-10-lost-tribes-of-israel.html
27. Phoenicia. 2013. Wikipedia. Retrieved October 23, 2013 from http://en.wikipedia.org/wiki/Phoenicia
28. Hartman, Paul V. 1995-2013. *The Phoenicians: Great Seafarers and More*. Hartman Website. Retrieved October 23, 2013 from http://www.naciente.com/essay64.htm
29. Mitchell, Antonio. 2014. Biblical meaning of numbers. *Biblical Resources Today*. Retrieved February 27, 2014 from http://www.christian-resources-today.com/biblical-meaning-of-numbers.html

END NOTES CHAPTERS 3-12

1. Steven M. Collins blog at wordpress.com. Published Sept 28, 2013. Ancient Coin Shows Phoenicians Present in North America retrieved October 18, 2013 from http://stevenmcollins.com/WordPress/?p=6527
2. Collins, Steven M. 2006-2013. The Missing Simeonites. Para 8. Retrieved October 21, 2013 from http://stevenmcollins.com/html/simeon.html
3. Jones, AHM. 1969. *Sparta*. 1994 Reprinted by Barnes and Nobel Inc.
4. Battle of Thermopylae. (2013, January 7). *New World Encyclopedia*. Retrieved October 21, 2013 from http://www.newworldencyclopedia.org/p/index.php?title=Battle_of_Thermopylae&oldid=966089.
5. I Maccabees 14. Retrieved October 21, 2013 from http://www.livius.org/maa-mam/maccabees/1macc14.html

6. Scythia. Retrieved October 23, 2013 from http://www.mapsofworld.com/world-ancient-history/scythia-map.html
7. Collins, Steven M. 2006-2013. *The Israelite Origins of the Scythians*. Retrieved October 16, 2013 from http://stevenmcollins.com/html/scythians.html
8. Several Scythian origins sources are quoted by Collins' article (source 7 above) placing the date of their appearance around 700 BC: The Encyclopedia Americana, historian of the Scythians, Tamara Talbot Rice, and "Assyrian documents place their appearance…on the shores of Lake Urmia [just south of Armenia] in the time of King Sargon (722-705 B.C.) a date which closely corresponds with that of the first establishment of the first group of Scythians in southern Russia." (ibid)
9. Jester, Jim. April 2010. As quotes from "Heirs of the Promise", Sheldon Emry, p. 17. Retrieved October 23, 2013 from http://fgcp.org/content/identifying-israel-part-4-0
10. Jester, Jim. April 2010. *Identifying Israel Part Four: The Scythian Connection*. Retrieved October 23, 2013 from http://fgcp.org/content/identifying-israel-part-4-0
11. Tamara Talbot Rice, *The Scythians*, pp. 19-20, 44
12. Hartman, Paul. 1995-2008. The Hartman Website. *The Parthinians*. Retrieved October 23, 2013 from http://www.naciente.com/essay5.htm
13. Rodriguez, Tommy. 2008-2013. *The Ancient World of the Carthaginians*. The Ancient World. Retrieved October 25, 2013 from http://www.theancientworld.net/civ/carthage.html
14. Rawlinson, *The Sixth Oriental Monarchy*, see "Preface (dated 1872), p. V. as quoted by Collins, Steven in *The Jews are Judah*. Retrieved October 28, 2013 from http://stevenmcollins.com/4_Reasons_the_Jews_are_Judah.pdf
15. Ibid. p. 19
16. Ibid p. 26
17. Collins, Steven. 2006-2013. *4 Reasons the Jews are Judah: The History of Asian Jews*. Para 5-6. retrieved October 28, 2013 from http://stevenmcollins.com/4_Reasons_the_Jews_are_Judah.pdf
18. Collins, Steven. (n.d.). Prophecy Updates and Commentary. *Lost Parthian City Found*. Retrieved October 28, 2013 from http://stevenmcollins.com/WordPress/?p=718
19. List of Parthian Kings. Wikipedia. Retrieved October 28, 2013 from http://en.wikipedia.org/wiki/List_of_Parthian_kings

20. Collins, Steven. 2006-2013. *My Viewpoints on the Modern day Location of the Tribe of Gad.* Retrieved October 29, 2013 from http://stevenmcollins.com/html/gad.html
21. Collins, Steven. 2007. Speech given in Portland Oregon. *Restoration of Forgotten History of Israel.* Minute 29.
22. Guisepi, Robert. (n.d.) The International History Project. *Prussia.* Retrieved October 30, 2013 from http://history-world.org/prussia.htm
23. *Reuben.* (n.d.) Brit-Am. Retrieved October 30, 2013 from http://britam.org/reuben.html
24. Salemi, Peter. (n.d.) British-Israel. *The Tribe of Reuben is Northern France.* Retrieved October 30, 2013 from http://www.british-israel.ca/Reuben.htm
25. Martlew, Valerie. (n.d.) *A Remnant of Israel in France.* Retrieved October 30, 2013 from http://www.ensignmessage.com/archives/israelremnant.html
26. Skelly, David. (n.d.) *Origin of France and its People.* Retrieved October 30, 2013 from http://www.originofnations.org/books,%20papers/origin_of_france_and_its_peoples.htm
27. Schrader, Eberhard & Whitehouse, Owen C. (n.d.) *The Cuneiform Inscriptions and the Old Testament,* (reprinted) vol. 1, Ulan Press. p. 177 as referred to by *The Land of the House of Omri.* Retrieved October 30, 2013 from http://www.destiny-worldwide.net/rcg/history/abp/america_.htm
28. Proud to be Irish. 1998-2006. The Celts. Retrieved October 31, 2013 from http://proud2beirish.com/Celtic-Ireland.htm
29. Collins, Steven. 2006-2013. *4 Reasons the Jews are Judah: Reason 3fulfillment of the Gen 49 Prophecy.* Para 6. Retrieved October 28, 2013 from http://stevenmcollins.com/4_Reasons_the_Jews_are_Judah.pdf
30. Grimaldi, A.B. 1885. The Queen's Royal Descent from King David the Psalmist. Retrieved November 3, 2013 from http://www.originofnations.org/Royals/queens%20descent/The%20Queen's%20Royal%20Descent%20from%20King%20David%20of%20Judah.htm
31. Davidiy, Yair. (n.d.) *Dan amongst the Celts.* Britam.org. Retrieved November 3, 2013 from http://www.british-israel.ca/Dan.htm
32. Davidiy, Yair. (n.d.) Britam.org. *Dan and the Serpent Way.* Retrieved November 3, 2013 from http://www.britam.org/dan3.html

33. Three sources that relate the Greeks and Israelites: 1. Hecataeus a 4th century BC Greek historian states Egypt "expelled all the [Israelite] aliens gathered together in Egypt. Of these, some, under their leaders Danuss and Cadmus, migrated into Greece; others into other regions, the greater part into Syria [Canaan]. Their leader is said to have been Moses, a man renowned for wisdom and courage, founder and legislator of the state" (*Fragmenta Historicorum Graecorum,* vol. 2, p. 385). 2. a 1965 book *Hellenosemetica* describes "two branches of the Danites ("Danunians" and "Danaans"), and shows that these people once occupied the island of Cyprus. It also mentions the Cyprian "tradition of the Danaan migration from the eastern Mediterranean" (pp. 14, 79). 3. "Professor Allen H. Jones (*Bronze Age Civilization—The Philistines and the Danites).* He traces the *Danaans,* a name that the famed Greek poet Homer often used for all Greeks, back to the Israelite tribe of *Dan."* All quotes are as written by Peter Salemi source 35 in this End Notes list.
34. *Collier's Encyclopedia.* 1950. Crowell, Collier and Macmillan. vol.17 p.434.
35. Salemi, Peter. (n.d.) *The Tribe of Dan is the Danes.* Retrieved October 24, 2013 from http://www.british-israel.ca/Dan.htm
36. Ghert-Zand, Renee. Oct 24, 2013. *The Times of Israel.* George dunked in Jordan River water. Retrieved October 25, 2013 from http://www.timesofisrael.com/george-dunked-in-jordan-river/?utm_source=The+Times+of+Israel+Daily+Edition&utm_campaign=077bd3d3e4-2013_10_25&utm_medium=email&utm_term=0_adb46cec92-077bd3d3e4-54458061
37. Collins, Steven. 1995. *Lost Ten Tribes of Israel, Found.* 1st Revised edition. CPA Books. p.412.
38. Collins, Steven. 1998-2006. *Why is Dan's Tribe Not Mentioned in Revelation 7?* Prophecy Updates and Commentary. Retrieved November 4, 2013 from http://stevenmcollins.com/WordPress/?p=6120
39. Lutheran statistics in Denmark retrieved November 4, 2013 from http://www.nationsencyclopedia.com/Europe/Denmark-RELIGIONS.html
40. Collins, Steven. 2008. *Benjamin is a Ravening Wolf?????* Prophecy Updates and Commentary. Wordpress. Retrieved November 5, 2013 from http://stevenmcollins.com/WordPress/?p=212

41. Collins, Steven. 1998-2006. *The Tribe of Benjamin: a Wolfpack from the North*. Retrieved November 5, 2013 from http://stevenmcollins.com/html/benjamin.html
42. Salemi, Peter. (n.d.) *The Tribe of Benjamin are the Normans*. British-Israel.ca. Retrieved November 5, 2013 from http://www.british-israel.ca/Benjamin.htm
43. Weeks, Andrew. 2011. *Flags of the Tribes of Israel*. Retrieved November 5, 2013 from http://www.crwflags.com/fotw/flags/il_tribe.html
44. Vesilind, Priit J. May 2000. In search of Vikings. *National Geographic*. pp.11-13.
45. Davidiy, Yair. 1993. *The Tribes*. Russell-Davis Publishers. Jerusalem. p.235. as quoted by Salemi, Peter in 42 above. Retrieved November 5, 2013 from http://www.british-israel.ca/Benjamin.htm
46. Rutherford, Adam. 1937. *Iceland's Great Inheritance*. Artesian Publishers, London England. footnote, p.37.
47. Salemi, Peter. The Tribe of Naphtali is Sweden and Norway. Retrieved November 7, 2013 from http://www.british-israel.ca/Naphtali.htm
48. Procopius (Book I. Ch 3-4). 6th Century Caesarea as quoted by Salemi, Peter in end Note 47. Retrieved November 7, 2013 from http://www.british-israel.ca/Naphtali.htm
49. Davidiy, Yair. 1993. *The Tribes*. Russell-Davis Publishers. Jerusalem.
50. Davidiy, Yair. (n.d.) Tribal Identifications: *Naphtali*. Retrieved November 7, 2013 from http://britam.org/naphtali.html
51. Salemi, Peter. Retrieved October 31, 2013 from http://www.british-israel.ca/Asher.htm
52. Orr, James. 1915. Oil. International Standard Bible Encyclopedia. Retrieved November 11, 2013 from http://www.biblestudytools.com/dictionary/oil/
53. Suessiones. (n.d.) Retrieved November 12, 2013 from http://en.wikipedia.org/wiki/Suessiones
54. Luxembourg. (n.d.) retrieved November 12 from http://en.wikipedia.org/wiki/Luxembourg
55. Collins, Steven M. (n.d.) Ephraim and Manasseh: Allies in the Modern World. Retrieved October 23, 2013 from http://stevenmcollins.com/Ephraim_and_Manasseh.pdf
56. Salemi, Peter. (n.d.) Ephraim is England and Her Commonwealth. Retrieved November 13, 2013 from http://www.british-israel.ca/Ephraim.htm

57. Collins, Steven M. 2005. *Israel's Tribes Today*. Bible Blessings. p.31-49.
58. Hannay, Herbert, *European and other Race Origins*, p. 232
59. Encyclopedia Britannica, Vol. 19, Heading entitled "Sarmatae," p. 1001 as quoted by Collins, Steven in *Israel's Tribes Today*.
60. Nesbit, Douglas. (n.d.) The Union Jack. The Prophetic Expositor. Retrieved November 14, 2013 from http://www.ensignmessage.com/archives/unionjack1.html
61. Collins, Steven. (n.d.) *The Tribe of Joseph in the Latter Days*. Retrieved November 3, 2013 from http://stevenmcollins.com/Joseph_in_the_Latter_Days.pdf
62. Margoliouth, Moses. 1818. *The History of the Jews in Great Britain*. P.12 & 387. As quoted by Yair Davidiy in *Spain and Britian*. Retrieved November 7, 2013 from http://www.ensignmessage.com/archives/spainandbrit.html
63. Davidiy, Yair. (n.d.) *Why the USA is Manasseh: A Summation*. Brit-Am. Retrieved November 18, 2013 from http://www.britam.org/USAManasseh.html
64. Davidiy, Yair. (n.d.) *Notes Concerning the British Empire*. Brit-Am. Retrieved November 18, 2013 from http://www.britam.org/BritishE.html#Prepared
65. Roe, Sue. (n.d.) *The Puritans*. Retrieved November 22, 2013 from http://genealogytoday.com/columns/recipes/tip13a.html
66. Roberts, Philip. (n.d.) *Ephraim and Manasseh: Role reversal refuted*. Ensign Message. Retrieved November 18, 2013 from http://www.ensignmessage.com/archives/ephraim.html
67. German Language. (n.d.) Retrieved November 22, 2013 from http://en.wikipedia.org/wiki/German_in_the_United_States
68. Ripley, William. 1899. *Races of Europe: A Sociological Study*. P.214
69. Collins, Steven M. 2002. *Parthia* (an excerpt of chapter 3). Retrieved November 22, 2013 from http://stevenmcollins.com/html/Parthia%20Excerpt.html
70. Issachar name meaning. Retrieved November 28, 2013 from http://www.abarim-publications.com/Meaning/Issachar.html
71. Collins, Steven M. (n.d.) Issachar in the Modern World. Retrieved November 29, 2013 from http://stevenmcollins.com/html/issachar.html
72. Salemi, Peter. (n.d.) Modern Day Issachar is Finland. Retrieved November 29, 2013 from http://www.british-israel.ca/Issachar.htm

73. Davidiy, Yair. (n.d.) Tribal Identification: Issachar. Retrieved November 29, 2013 from http://britam.org/issachar.html
74. Jewish Encyclopedia. 1906. Tribe of Issachar. Retrieved November 29, 2013 from http://www.jewishencyclopedia.com/articles/8335-issachar-tribe-of
75. Uittenbogaard, Arie. (n.d.) *Zebulun*. Abarim Publications. Retrieved December 11, 2013 from http://www.abarim-publications.com/Meaning/Zebulun.html
76. Wikipedia. (n.d.) "Port of Rotterdam. Retrieved December 11, 2013 from http://en.wikipedia.org/wiki/Port_of_Rotterdam
77. Collins, Steven. 1993. Lost Ten Tribes Found. (same as source 37)
78. Salemi, Peter. (n.d.) *Zebulun*. British Israel. Retrieved December 11, 2013 from http://www.british-israel.ca/Zebulun.htm
79. Koppejan, Helene. 2009. *Strange Parallel*, ninth edition. Artesian Publishers. As quoted by Salemi in source immediately above.
80. Salemi, Peter. (n.d.) British Israel. The Tribe of Levi. Retrieved December 4, 2013 from http://www.british-israel.ca/Levi.htm
81. *Psaltry*. 2010. Yahweh's Restoration Ministry. Strong's Concordance 5035 "Nabel"
82. Young, Patrick. Genetic Testing. Retrieved December 8, 2013 from http://creationists.org/patrickyoung/article12.html
83. Koniuchowsky, Rabbi Moshe Joseph. 2011. The role of Levites in Israel's 2-house restoration. Hebraic Heritage Ministries International. Retrieved December 12, 2013 from http://www.hebroots.org/hebrootsarchive/0105/0105s.html
84. Collins, Steven. Nov 2013. Ancient Israel knew the earth was round. Retrieved December 12, 2013 from http://stevenmcollins.com/WordPress/?cat=1
85. Greenspan, Michael. 2006. Against all odds, Israel survives. Questar Studios video presentation.
86. Collins, Steven. Nov 2008. Blog Q&A Origins of the Nations. Retrieved December 16, 2013 from http://stevenmcollins.com/WordPress/?p=351
87. Donnely, Jeffery. (n.d.) Who were the wise men? Netplaces.com. Retrieved December 15, 2013 from http://www.netplaces.com/bible-history/unwrapping-the-nativity/who-were-the-wise-men.htm
88. *Zodiac*. (n.d.) Asis Internet. Retrieved December 16, 2013 from http://www.asis.com/users/stag/zodiac.html

89. world maps resource: by Thomas Lessman http://www.worldhistorymaps.info/
90. 90.Salemi, Peter. (n.d.) Manasseh is the United States of America. Retrieved April 2, 2014 from http://www.british-israel.ca/Manasseh.htm
91. Retrieved June 3, 2014 from http://www.germanroots.com/2000.html
92. Retrieved July 29, 2014 from http://www.hyperhistory.com/online_n2/History_n2/a.html
93. Retrieved July 29, 2014 from http://www.hyperhistory.com/online_n2/History_n2/a.html

ALSO AVAILABLE FROM THIS AUTHOR

Paperback or Kindle version of the original *Israel Basics.: What Every Christian Should Know*. This 240+ page book covers the history, prophecy, some culture and language basics of the Chosen People. A great foundation for anyone, and it can be used as a small group study guide.

Available on Amazon.com
Paper copy ISBN#978-0692014400
Kindle ISBN# 978-0-9903059-27

This book goes *Beyond the Basics* into further detail on the Hebrew language, the Feasts of the Lord, the history of the Church and the Jews and the origins of the Holocaust. It is a great follow up for anyone who wants to know more about their Hebrew Roots. It can be used individually or in a group study.

Available on Amazon.com
Paper copy ISBN# 978-0-9903059-0-3
Kindle ISBN# 978-0-9903059-3-4

www.ingramcontent.com/pod-product-compliance
Lightning Source LLC
Chambersburg PA
CBHW070146100426
42743CB00013B/2829